A GLOSSARY OF

IRISH SLANG

AND UNCONVENTIONAL LANGUAGE

ALSO AVAILABLE

Louis Bell
POPULAR IRISH POETRY

Laurence Flanagan
IRISH PROVERBS

John Grenham
IRISH ANCESTORS

Padraic O'Farrell
ANCIENT IRISH LEGENDS
IRISH CUSTOMS
IRISH FAIRY TALES
IRISH FOLK CURES
IRISH SAINTS
IRISH SURNAMES

Dáithí Ó hÓgáin
IRISH SUPERSTITIONS

Diarmaid Ó Muirithe
IRISH WORDS & PHRASES

A GLOSSARY OF IRISH SLANG AND UNCONVENTIONAL LANGUAGE

DIARMAID Ó MUIRITHE

Gill & Macmillan

Gill & Macmillan Ltd
Hume Avenue, Park West, Dublin 12
with associated companies throughout the world
www.gillmacmillan.ie

0 7171 3728 7
Original text design by
Identikit Design Consultants, Dublin
Print origination by Carole Lynch
Printed and bound by Nørhaven Paperback A/S, Denmark

This book is typeset in 10/15pt Adobe Garamond.

The paper used in this book comes from the wood pulp of managed forests. For every tree felled, at least one tree is planted, thereby renewing natural resources.

A CIP catalogue record for this book is available from the British Library.

1 3 5 4 2

IN MEMORIAM RICHARD WALL,

AND FOR

TERRY DOLAN,

CONSERVATORS OF THE 'LIRYC AND

THEMODIOUS SOFT AGLO IRIS

OF THE VALS'.

CONTENTS

INTRODUCTION

Slang, according to Collins English Dictionary, is 'Vocabulary, idiom etc., that is not appropriate to the standard form of a language or to formal contexts, may be restricted as to social status or distribution, and is characteristically more metaphorical and transitory than standard language.'

Cant, of which there are many examples in this little book, is defined in the same work as 'specialised vocabulary of a particular group such as thieves, journalists or lawyers'.

Oxford has this: 'Slang: (a) The special vocabulary used by any set of persons of a low or disreputable character; language of a low and vulgar type. (Now merged in cant.) (b) The special vocabulary or phraseology of a particular class or profession, the cant or jargon of a certain class or period. (c) Language of a highly colloquial type, considered as below the level of standard educated speech, and consisting of new words or of words employed in some special sense.'

I have added some good dialect words to this collection of slang and cant, words of a highly colloquial type, and, unfortunately, considered by many to be below the level of educated speech.

Slang has had both its detractors and its champions. Alan Bennett in his 1981 *Cold Sweat,* wrote: 'There is something suspect (and potentially ridiculous) about those in the vanguard of slang.' Robert Burchfield in *The English Language* (1985) called slang 'dustbin language'. Anthony Burgess in his 1992 *A Mouthful of Air*, described slang rather well, I think: 'The word slang is vague and its etymology obscure. It suggests the slinging of odd stones or dollops of mud at the windows of the stately home of linguistic decorum.' Chesterton loved slang. In his essay *In Defence of Slang* (1901) he claimed that 'All slang is metaphor, and all metaphor is poetry.' Galsworthy agreed: 'Slang is vigorous and apt. Probably most of our vital words were once slang.' George Eliot said, or at least one of her characters said, in *Middlemarch*, that 'Correct English is the slang of prigs who write history and essays. And the strongest slang of all is the slang of poets.'

Indeed poets were among the greatest defenders of slang. Our greatest dialect poet, James Joyce, revelled in it; Carl Sandburg said that 'Slang is a language that rolls up its sleeves, spits on its hands and goes to work.' That prompted A.P. Herbert to remark that he thought of slang as 'a language that is always taking its trousers off ...'

Walt Whitman was the most eloquent of all admirers of slang. In *Slang in America* (1885) he wrote this: 'Slang, profoundly considered is the lawless germinal element, below all words and sentences, and behind all poetry, and proves a certain freedom and perennial rankness and Protestantism in speech ... Slang is the wholesome fermentation or eructation of those processes, eternally active in language, by which froth and specks are thrown up, mostly to pass away; though occasionally to settle and permanently crystallise.'

Slang hasn't been neglected by Irish lexicographers. We are indebted to Bernard Share and his *Slanguage*; to the various works of the late Richard Wall; to the works of T.P. Dolan and Séamus Moylan; to William Lutton and his *Montiaghisms* from the banks of Lough Neagh; to Seamus Mac Connell and his little books of Derry speech; to Seán Beecher and his *Dictionary of Cork Slang*, to C.I. Macafee's *Concise Ulster Dictionary*; to Willie O'Kane from Dungannon and his collection of Ulster words, *You Don't Say*; to a great teacher, Mrs Rae McIntyre, and her pupils in Ballyrashane School, near Coleraine, who gave us the marvellous *Some Handlin'*; to the anonymous Tuam schoolboys who gave us the collection *A Beginner's Dictionary of Tuam Slang* in *The Great Tuam Annual*. I mustn't forget all those who sent me words to my column in *The Irish Times*; and to those people who collected words for their various parish annuals throughout Ireland.

For the cant words, thanks to my friend, teacher Pádraig Mac Gréine, or Paddy Green, or

Master Green as he is called by the people of Ballinalee, Co. Longford, and in the following text. His great collection of Shelta words are incorporated in Macalister's *The Secret Languages of Ireland*, published in 1937. He is still hale and hearty, teaching Traveller children their secret language, at the age of 103. My thanks too, to Mrs Annie Wall and her family, and to Mr Miley Connors, both of no fixed abode, but considered by themselves to be Wexford people.

Tolle, lege. I hope you enjoy this little sampler.

TERMS USED IN THIS GLOSSARY

Anglo-French: The French used in Medieval England

Anglo-Norman: The form of Anglo-French used by the Norman conquerors

Germanic: The Indo-European language from which most of the modern languages of Europe developed

Hiberno-English: An umbrella term for the various strands of English spoken in Ireland

Indo-European: The parent language of most of the languages spoken now in Europe and northern India. Indo-European developed c. 4000 BC

Latin: The language of the Romans until c. 200 AD

Late Latin: The Latin spoken from c. 200 to 600 AD

Medieval Latin: The Latin used in the Christian liturgy and in literature from c. 600 to 1500

Middle Dutch: The language spoken between c. 1100 and 1500

Middle English: The language spoken from c. 1150 to 1500

Middle French: The French spoken between c. 1300 and 1600

Middle High German: The form of German spoken in the south of Germany, where the land is higher than in the north, from c. 1100 to 1500. Modern German is descended from *Middle High German*

Middle Low German: The German spoken elsewhere than in southern Germany, c. 1100 to 1500

Old English: The type of English spoken until c. 1150

Old French: The type of French spoken until c. 1300

Old High German: The language spoken in southern Germany until c. 1100

Old Norse/Old Icelandic: The common language of Scandinavia and Iceland until c. 1350

Old North French: The dialects of *Old French* spoken in Normandy and Picardy

Sanskrit: The ancient sacred language of India, the oldest known member of the Indo-European family, in which the extensive Hindu literature from the Vedas downward is composed. It dates from c. 1200 BC

Scots: The form of English spoken by the inhabitants of the Lowlands of Scotland

Shelta: The secret language of the Irish Travellers. Also called *Sheldru, Minker's Tawrie, Tinker's Cant* and *Gammon*

Alamach

This is Shelta for milk. There are many recorded variants, *elima*, *elimoch*, *alemnoch*, *alamuck* among them. Master Green gives *alamach grut* for buttermilk; gruth is Irish for curds. He also recorded *alamach ly*, fresh milk. *Ly* here is a problem. I have no doubt, however, and neither has Master Green, that *alamach* is from the Irish *leamhnacht*, new milk.

Ardhughs

A lady from Kingscourt gave me this word. This is how she glossed it: 'The old people used to say, when they made excuses for youngsters' high-jinks, "Ah sure, don't heed the poor gossons, it's only the ardhughs."' The *Concise Ulster Dictionary* has: '*ardhughs*, noun, plural, antics, capers, origin unknown'.

Surely this is the Irish *ardú* with the English plural ending. Ó Dónaill's dictionary defines *ardú* as excitement, as well as the verbal noun of *ardaigh*, rise. Now consider this: in my long-lost youth I mentioned to an old woman I knew in Glenmore, south Kilkenny, that Miss Marilyn Monroe was the sexiest woman I had ever seen in my life, and I had begun to tell her about that song in *Some Like it Hot* when she cut in to enquire whether she should send her husband to the pictures to see would Marilyn give the oul' lad *th'ardoo* as well. Origin unknown, eh?

Banjaxed

This is a real Dublin slang word for 'totally destroyed'. Flann O'Brien has it in *At-Swim-Two-Birds*: 'Here is his black heart sitting there as large as life in the middle of the pulp of his banjaxed corpse.' Beckett has it as well in *Waiting for Godot* in the 1956 edition of the play: 'Lucky might get going all of a sudden. Then we'd be banjaxed.' But in the 1954 edition he has *bollocksed* instead of *banjaxed*, for some reason. Thanks to Bernard Share for spotting that. My friend Terry Wogan has found everlasting fame in having his name associated with banjaxed in the *Oxford Dictionary*: in 1972 he announced on BBC radio that he was 'out to banjax the bookies'.

Banners

This is Tuam, Co. Galway slang for a bag of chips. From the potatoes called Arran Banners. Perhaps I should at this point say something about Tuam slang. In 1991 I was sent a copy of *The Great Tuam Annual*, a publication of the local Lions Club, printed in aid of local charities. It contained an article entitled *A Beginner's Dictionary of Tuam Slang*, a highly amusing and informative piece. The editor gave special recognition to certain unnamed students of St Jarlath's College. I, too, am indebted to them in this little book.

Beater

Pronounced *baythur*, this is a Cork word for penis. Seán Beecher gave us the word in his *Dictionary of Cork Slang*.

Beoir

Traveller's cant for a woman. *Beoir a kena* means woman of the house. *Beoir lugail* is a wailing woman. *Beoir ar mislo* is a wandering woman. *Beoir srigo*, a queen. *Beoir swudar* or *beoir swudal*, a 'high woman', a lady. *Beoir* is thought to be a distortion of Irish *bean*, a woman.

Beure

This is a slang word for a girl, a young woman, used in Tuam. The Shelta (or Sheldru or Minker's Tawrie, or Tinker's Cant) is *beoir*. This is the Irish word *bean*, a woman, distorted out of recognition.

Birdlime

Birdlime is Tuam rhyming slang for 'time'. 'Lamp the birdlime; let's skirt', is Tuamspeak for 'look at the time; let's go quickly.'

Blánóg/blawnogue

This is Shelta for a cow. *Blánóg* is one of the words Master Green collected. It is from the Irish *bleánach*, a milking.

Bleeze

You'll find lobsters in the most unexpected places, the Irish saying goes; and it was indeed an unexpected pleasure to hear of an old Wexfordwoman from the Campile district who used the very old word *bleeze* as she warned her granddaughter about the dangers of wearing short skirts. *Bleeze* means bladder.

This word was new to me, but I found it, spelled *bleaze* – not that that matters – in a Pembrokeshire dialect dictionary. Now you don't need to be told that there is an old link between Pembrokeshire and south Wexford, so I suppose one shouldn't be surprised that a word as old as this is to be found here in this Anglo-Norman stronghold. *Bleeze/bleaze* represents the Old English *blaese*, bladder; Middle High German *blase*, and Old High German *blasa*.

Blight

A Tuam blight is a dolt, an idiot; the pox. My source for all Tuam slang words, the *Beginner's Dictionary* already quoted, gives a context: 'That sham (q.v.) is pure blight.'

Bluemouldy/bluemoulded

This slang phrase is quite common. It means in dire need of something, such as a drink. Joyce's use of the phrase is echoed today in pubs all over Ireland; in *Ulysses* he has: 'I was blue mouldy for the want of that pint.' Somerville and Ross, in *Some Experiences of an Irish R.M.* have: 'I was thinkin' you were blue moulded for want of a batin.' *Mouldy* is, of course, pronounced to rhyme with 'fouled'. I can't even guess as to the word's origin; it doesn't seem to me to be related to *mouldy*, drunk (q.v.).

Bowsey

Dublin slang for a hooligan, a gutty, a gurrier [q.v]. Used by many of Dublin's great writers, O'Casey among them. O'Casey, in *The Plough and the Stars* has: 'Here, out you go, me little bowsey.' Joyce, in *Dubliners* has: 'Sure, amn't I never done at the drunken bowsy ever since he left school.' The word may be from *booze*.

Box the fox

A Dublin slang phrase, for stealing apples and pears from orchards. Eamonn Mac Thomáis has this in his memoir, *Janey Mack, Me Shirt is Black*: 'Suddenly I began to love skipping and had no time for football or boxing the fox.' Of unknown origin.

Bras

This is another of Master Green's words collected from his Traveller friends. It means food. O'Reilly's Irish dictionary give *bras*, 'bread, means of living', from an unspecified 'old glossary'.

Bravan

A Traveller's word for corn or grain. It is also used to translate the Traveller surname Oates. It is a distortion of the Irish *arbhar*, corn. Mrs Annie Wall gave me the word in Co. Wicklow.

Brock/Brockman

Scraps of food; broken victuals; leftover food. *Brock* was fed to pigs. In Ulster towns the *brockman* used to go around in a cart collecting the food; he then sold it to the pig fatteners. I have to thank Seamus Mac Connell for the word.

Brock is Scots. Kelly's collection of Scots proverbs (1724) refers to a person having 'neither stock nor brock'. Tennant's *Papistry*, published in 1824, has: 'Piper Jock ... Picked up the banes that lay like brock.' The ultimate origin of the word is the Old English *broccan* (dative plural), fragments.

Budgie

'A young person of the female gender' is how the *Beginner's Dictionary of Tuam Slang* glosses *budgie*. From the bird of that name, I assume.

Buff/Buffer

'A countryman, a rustic fellow' (Tuam). On the evidence of the *Beginner's Dictionary*, countrymen were not highly regarded by the townies.

Bugle

Dublin slang for an erection. Used more than once by Roddy Doyle in his novels. 'I've a bugle here yeh could blow in, 'melda,' is from *The Van*.

Bugler

This is almost certainly a schoolboy's amusing word for a burger, 'meat fixed between two buns', as described in the Tuam slang glossary.

Burry, buri

Shelta adjectives meaning great, fine, beautiful. Of uncertain origin. Macalister speculates that the origin may be Romani *baro* in which the first vowel is long; in the Shelta words, however, this vowel is short. There are variants of Master Green's words: *bura, buri, baro, bare, bawrie* among them.

Burying the soldier

Eddie O'Sullivan, a former detective, gave me this Garda Síochána slang phrase. He heard it on one of his first postings, when a sergeant assigned him the unpleasant duty of burying the soldier. It transpired that it meant digging buckets of clay from a neighbouring field and covering the contents of the barracks dry latrine with it.

Butty

There are two Dublin slang *butties*. One is a bosom companion, often a boozing companion; a co-worker. O'Casey, in *Juno and the Paycock*, has: 'The foreman on the job is an oul' butty o' Joxer's.'

The other *butty* is a sandwich. Roddy Doyle in *The Snapper* has: 'I'll butter a few slices, will I? For butties.'

Both butties are also in English slang. We find the first in Grose's *History of the Vulgar Tongue* in 1790; the second is defined by the *English Dialect Dictionary* as 'a slice of bread and butter; also bread spread with treacle, sugar, etc.' Common slang throughout England.

Cackler

This is a Tuam chicken. You may buy a *cackler's corie* in the chip shops of that pleasant town – a leg of chicken. *Cackler* is Shelta for a duck, also an egg. I don't know the origin of *corie*, I'm afraid.

Caidogues

Tuam schoolboy slang for the testicles, or to quote their own gloss, 'male organs not usually seen in public'. *Caid* is a word for a football in Kerry. It is the same word as Old English *cod*, a bag. A patent medicine advertised in 1527 claimed that it was good for 'mannes yardes and coddes'; a sort of Tudor Viagra, you might say. *Caideogs* are 'stones used for pelting' in Shelta.

Cake

Here is another example of the townsman's lexicon of impolite terms for those who live in the countryside. *Cake* is Tuamspeak for a farmer.

Cane

This is a Tuam word for a house. *Cane* is from Shelta. *Kén, kéna* and *cian* are words for a house. *Beoir a kéna* means 'woman of the house'. *Shédes kén* (shades cane) is the Traveller's expression for a police barracks. They call a big house *cian tóim*; a little house, *bini kena*; a public house, *kén gáter*; a brothel is *kén spurko*. The Shelta words are thought to be from Romani *kér*.

Cawlra

I was given this word by the late J.F. Killeen, a Classical scholar and a gentleman who adorned University College Galway for many years. He heard the word in a Galway pub, used, not by a Traveller, but by a labourer from Rahoon direction. He was talking about a vicious murder that was in the news, and he explained that a woman had been stabbed with a kitchen *cawlra*.

Cawlra is Shelta for a knife. A Traveller well versed in the cant might have said *cálra sharku* for a knife of that sort, or for a saw. It is thought that *cawlra* is from the Romani *curi*.

Chairwheeze

This is Tuam schoolboy slang. It is, according to the *Beginner's Dictionary of Tuam Slang*, a rude noun meaning 'the act of passing wind either gently or vigorously'.

Change yourself

Derry-speak for put on new clothes.

Chant

A Tuam slang word for a song, or a tune on a musical instrument. You might hear the following in a Tuam public house, *A tome chant for a skate, Sham*? See *tome*, *skate* and *Sham* below, and you'll understand.

Child

In many parts of Ireland and southern England a *child* is a female infant; in both places the question *Is it a boy or a child?* may be heard. This is a relic of the great age of the Tudors. In *The Winter's Tale* the following is heard from the old shepherd: 'Mercy on't, a barne: a very pretty barne! a boy or a child, I wonder?'

Chitty-face

A woman from Kilkeel, Co. Down, who is the wife of a trawler skipper, told me in a hostelry in Kilmore Quay, Co. Wexford, that the term *chitty-face* was used in her schooldays by brats teasing fellow-pupils who were thin. In those days, fat kids weren't taunted as much as they are nowadays, she said; now thin is in, as they say.

'Chitty-face, chitty-face, skinnymalink', the young bullies would sing out.

Nathan Bailey's dictionary of 1750 was the first to include *chitty-face*. He defined it as 'a meagre, starveling young child'. The *English Dialect Dictionary* has *chitty-faced*, 'a baby-faced or a lean-faced person, having the face of a *chit*, a contemptuous word for a child or a small girl'. A Cornish dictionary gives *chitter-faced* as if from *chitter*, thin.

All these words are corruptions of *chichevache*, a medieval monster who devoured only patient wives, and being, therefore, in a chronic state of starvation was made a by-word for leanness. The monster's name was formed from Old English and French;

chiche, meagre, starving, and *vache*, a cow. In Lydgate's *Ballad of Chichevache and Bicorne* there is this: 'Chichevache this is my name;/Hungry, megre, sklenrde and leene,/To show my body I have grete shame/For hunger I fele so grete teene;/On me no fatnesse will be seene;/By cause that pasture I find none/Therefor I am but skyn and boon.'

Chaucer warns women not to be like Griselde, 'Lest Chichevache you swalwe in hir entraille.'

Chiúch

I have given the spelling of the Shelta word as I have heard it from Miley Connors, a Traveller from Wexford. *Chiúch kuldrum* are bedclothes. *Chiúch* is concocted from the Irish *éadach*.

Choice/Choicer me Grocer

The word *choice* in Tuam slang means 'nothing'. *Choicer me grocer* means 'absolutely nothing at all'. And if you asked me where the terms originated I would have to say truthfully that I could offer choicer me grocer about the matter.

Chuck

This is a Tuam slang word for nourishment, sustenance, food. Of uncertain origin, which must be said of most slang words.

Clem

This is a word from both Monaghan and Cavan. The late Peadar Ó Casaide once sent it to me. He glossed it as 'a lout; a low-down hooligan'.

That this is from Scots I have no doubt, but strangely neither *The Concise Scots Dictionary* nor the *English Dialect Dictionary* have it as a noun. They both have it as an adjective meaning low, untrustworthy, mean; and both say that it is a slang word used mostly by schoolboys. Origin unknown.

Clift

This noun, which means an idiot, a mentally unbalanced person, is, it seems, confined to the north of Ireland. If a clift is thought to be a bit strong in describing a person, there are degrees one might try; for example, a *three-quarter clift* is close to being a complete idiot; a *quarter clift* is a simpleton. And if one wants to emphasise another's utter idiocy, one might call him or her *the two ends of a clift*. The *Concise Ulster Dictionary* says that clift is possibly the same word as Standard English past participle *cleft*.

Clissy

Séamas Ó Saothraí, scholar, lexicographer and biographer, gave me the Westmeath word *clissy*.

It was used endearingly when speaking of a young child: 'Aren't you the little clissy!' *Clissy* is an anglicised form of the Irish *cleasaí*, a trickster.

Cockseye

Or should this be spelled *cock's eye*? It is, whatever way you spell it, a ring around the moon in south-east Wexford. It is a sign of bad weather.

Coddle

'Cuddle up in coddlepot' sang Joyce in *Finnegans Wake*. An Australian chef once wrote to me about the word, and all I could tell her was that the ingredients of his Dublin concoction are rashers, sausages, tripe, onions, potatoes, milk and seasonings. *Coddle* was a traditional Saturday night meal in Dublin since the eighteenth century. As a verb meaning to stew, it was first used in literature by Ben Jonson in *Every man In His Humour* in 1598: 'Taking in all the young wenches that pass by and coddling every kernel of fruit from them.'

The origin of the word is uncertain. Oxford has doubts about a suggested north French *caudeler*, to warm, heat gently, for the very good reason that the form has never been found.

Coffee and crames

In the 1950s I remember various unkind epithets being hurled (if you'll pardon the pun) by country spectators at teams that were based in towns. Never mind that many of the town teams were composed mainly of rural migrants; they were the butt of taunts from the sons of toil who insisted that they must be cissies, pansies or popinjays to be living in towns. And so they were given names such as *Coffee and crames*; *Bread-and-tay boys*; *After you, Margarets*; *Butterflies*.

Bread-and-tay boys reminds me of the old Tudor epithet *toast-and-butter* for an effeminate man. Beaumont and Fletcher in *Wit Without Money* have: 'They love young toasts and butter, Bow Bell suckers.' And Falstaff in *Henry IV* says: 'I press me none but such toasts and butter, with hearts in their bellies no bigger than pins' heads.'

Cog

This verb, as every schoolboy knows, means to cheat by illicit copying in an examination. The word is very common in Ireland, and it is found in Scotland as well as in Cheshire and Sussex, and Master Shakespeare from Warwickshire also used it.

Cogging, participial adjective, cheating, deceiving, is common in Scotland. Sir Walter Scott has: 'None of your cogging gibberish – tell me truly', in *The Bride of Lammermoor*. Shakespeare uses the verb in *Richard III*: 'I cannot flatter and speak fair,/Smile in men's faces, smooth, deceive and cog.'

This was originally a dice-playing term, of unknown origin.

Comer

This good word came to me from Dr James Clarke of Rathcoole, Co. Dublin. One of his patients had complained that whatever tablets he had previously prescribed for her hadn't taken the comer out of her discomfort.

Comer, also found in the dialect dictionaries of Scotland, England and Ulster as *cummer, cumber* and *cummar,* is defined as 'inconvenience, trouble'. The Scots poet Dunbar, writing about 1510, has 'Sic hunger, sic cummer within this land was nivir hard nor scene,' and Tindale's translation of St Luke, written about 1526, has: 'Martha was combred about moche servynge.'

Dr Clarke's word is probably Germanic in origin. I had thought it related to encumbrance, which may be from Old French *encombrer*, to encumber; but the Dutch has *kommer*, distress, trouble, sorrow, and the German has *Kummer*, sorrow, grief, trouble. All the great dictionaries say that *comer* is from *encombrer*; one, *The World Book Dictionary*, says that the Old French word may be from the Late Latin *cumbrus*, a mysterious word of unknown origin. Odds on, I'd say that *cumbrus* has a Germanic antecedent somewhere.

Coof

Coof is a good word for an eejit. You'll hear it in parts of Antrim, and it came across the Moyle a long time ago. Ramsay, a fine Scots poet whose works are now sadly neglected, has the line 'Let coofs their cash be clinking.' In a poem about drinking Robert Burns tut-tuts about the way 'fumblin *cuifs* their dearies slight'. He reverts to the more usual *coof* in *For a' That*: 'Tho' hundreds worship at his word, he's but a coof for a' that.'

Both the *Ballymena Observer*, that invaluable source of Antrim words (1892), and W.H. Patterson's glossary of 1890 have the word. Patterson's gloss is 'A lout, an awkward, clownish fellow'. In Scotland a coof might also mean a man who does what is regarded to be a woman's work; a cotquean, in other words.

As to origin, the great Oxford hedges its bets here. It says the form corresponds to an earlier *cof*, which might be identical with Middle English *cofe*, now *cove*, slang for a fellow, but the words show little agreement in sense. It also says identity with

Scots *coffe*, also *cofe*, *coif*, merchant, hawker, has been suggested, but here the phonology presents difficulty. Better, in this case, to hide behind 'of obscure origin', for safety sake, methinks.

Coonick/supercoonick

Coonick is defined in the Tuam slang glossary as 'a person who performs religious rites. *Supercoonick* is a person of higher authority', a bishop, I suppose. Origin? I haven't a clue.

Cope

Máire Nic Mhaoláin, scholar and bibliophile, has sent me many's the good word from Co. Down in her time; *cope* is one of them. Picture the scene: a poor mountainy man, stressed out by the worries and cares of this cruel world, decides to visit his physician. One phrase he wouldn't use is 'I can't cope, doctor', for the simple reason that *to cope* means to evacuate the bowels, where the mountains of Mourne sweep down to the sea.

Crappin

This is an Ulster word, courtesy of Willie O'Kane from Dungannon. It means the stomach or crop. Thus spake Mr O'Kane: 'Some years ago an Englishman, on entering a Co. Derry hostelry and informing the proprietor that he'd cycled from Larne through a snowstorm and hadn't eaten for several hours, was bemused by his host's pronouncement that "You be to have a right empty crappin on you by now."'

Crappin is Scots in origin. Hogg's contemporary from Galloway, Nicholson, wrote of a 'theatre nymph in borough town' who 'disclosed the beauties of her crappin'.

Creel

A slang verb this from Galway. It means to beat, thrash, somebody. I've no idea where it originated, nor have I seen it in any book on British slang.

Croaked

A Galway slang adjective. It is, I'm assured, still used by schoolboys in Tuam. It means feeble, faulty, rotten.

Crolusc

A Shelta word meaning hunger, a distortion of Irish *ocras*. The Irish sentence *Tá ocras orm*, 'there is hunger on me, I am hungry,' may be rendered *tá crolusc a mwilsha* in Shelta. Mrs Wall, my Wexford Traveller friend, had this; so has Master Green from Ballinalee, Co. Longford.

Cuk (on)

This is a word I heard in Wexford when I was young. You could, in certain shops, get the *Champion* or the *Hotspur*, the main literary nourishment of our youth, *on cuk*, if you hadn't the price on the day. *Cuk* is Shelta. It is undoubtedly distorted from the English slang 'tick'.

Culchie

A Dublin person's dismissive word for a countryman. The word's etymology has long been the subject of debate. I tend to agree with those who say that the word is a shortening of *agricultural*. A friend of mine, the late Risteard B. Breatnach, the UCD linguist, used to say that it was originally coined by Dublin girls who used to frequent 'hops' run by the Agricultural Students' Society of UCD (the *Ags*) in the 1930s.

Cundick

In the south-east they use the word *cundick* for a conduit. There is a passageway near the quays in New Ross called Cundick Lane, and the name has given rise to many's the asinine proposal for a name-change down through the years. *Cundick* is an old dialect word for 'conduit', and it's from the

Middle English *cundit*, itself from the Old French *condut*, from Medieval Latin *conductus*.

Curse of Colmcille (on you)

This is a jocular kind of an Ulster curse which hasn't travelled south. It is said to a person who puts on a shoe and a sock before putting on the two socks first. It's a translation of the Irish *mallacht Cholm Cille*, which was a curse that befell the poor man in his youth when he had to flee from his enemies wearing only one shoe.

Cutcher

This is Mrs Wall's Shelta word for a cat. Master Green has it from Longford Travellers as well.

Dályon

The Traveller's word for God. There are other recorded variants. *Dályon swudr!* God above! Not all agree that the word is a distortion of the Irish *Dia*, as the *d* is not palatalised.

Damnify

A northern verb this, which means to ruin something; to damage something badly. I first heard the word used in Co. Down, by a man who was telling how a horse he had bought kicked the stable door to pieces. Tennant's viciously sectarian *Papistry*, published in 1827, in Fife, Scotland, suggests: 'The iron-geddock, swerd or spear, To damnifie the Scarlet Lady'. It is now confined to Ulster, Scotland and the northern counties of England. It is from Old French *damnifier*.

Dandilly

Glossed in W.H. Lutton's *Montiaghisms* as 'A young person who through over-indulgence is become feeble in body, or pettish in temper, or both'. Apparently the word is Scots, but of unknown origin.

Dead Cut

I have no idea where this slang term came from. Lutton has it in his *Montiaghisms* (1927), and he defines it thus: 'To be at or on the Dead Cut is to use the most strenuous and incessant exertion, whether voluntary or otherwise.'

Dick (to keep)

This is an Antrim slang expression for 'to keep a lookout'. W.H. Patterson has it in his glossary compiled towards the end of the nineteenth century. Brian Moore uses it in *Lies of Silence*: 'We should be keepin' dick.'

Dilsy

I often wonder just how many pejorative words we have for women of whom we do not approve. A *dilsy* is a good Ulster noun for a woman who is a social climber, with a fondness for name-dropping. Think of Mrs Hyacinth Bucket; now there's a real dilsy. As to origin, nobody has a clue.

Dinger/going, or doing, his dinger

A phrase commonly used in Ireland is 'He was going (or doing) his dinger.' A Dublin woman glossed it for me as 'He was going berserk, or at least he had lost his cool.' An Armagh woman I know glossed it for me as 'He was travelling at a dangerous speed.' I heard it in Wicklow, said of a visiting motorcyclist who seemed to think that rural roads are T.T. courses. Said a Delgany man to me: 'He was going his dinger; he couldn't take the bend and he cleared the ditch and ended up in the next parish.' This was said with a certain amount of glee, as the motorcyclist was unharmed although his machine was ruined.

Well, the phrase seems to have a few shades of meaning. It may be regarded as slang nowadays, but it has a long pedigree. It came here with the boys in the longships; it's from the Old Norse *dengja*, to hammer.

Dingleycooch

This is an Ulster expression for a very remote place. It comes from the Kerry town, *Dingle*, in Irish *Daingean Uí Chúis*, which to, let's say, Antrim Glensmen, where the expression is still used, must once have seemed like the ends of the earth, the back of godspeed. To be sent to, or to go to Dingleycooch meant to be sent to Coventry; to be excluded from other people's company. I see that many of the Ulster glossaries of the nineteenth century have the expression.

Dirty Arabs and Bloody Turks

I am sorry to relate, gentle readers, that Cork city school children – ah, and sometimes their parents too – have been heard to use these epithets to fling at people they regard as yobs. Echoes of the speech of the Munster Fusiliers, some would say.

Dixie

Mary O'Callaghan wrote to me from London to tell me that her father, a Corkman, always called a kettle a *dixie*. A futher note from the lady explained that her father was an old soldier.

Dixie is certainly a soldier's word and it reached Cork courtesy of the Munster Fusiliers, from India. There it meant a kettle or pot, made of iron, and used to make either tea or stew. It's in Hindi as *degchi*, and that word was adopted once upon a time from the Persian *degcha*, diminutive of *deg*, an iron pot, cauldron, or kettle.

Dog/Black Dog

In Cork this was an unpaid bill, or a slate not cleaned in a public house. It could also mean a bad cheque. Beecher has it in his book on Cork slang: 'He left a black dog after him.' I think he was right in saying that it originated in the early eighteenth century. Partridge says that it was current c. 1705-25, recorded first in Luttrell, 1706, as quoted in John Ashton's *Social Life in the Age of Queen Anne* (1882); and last in Swift's *Drapier's Letters*, 1724. Alexander Smith's *Highwaymen*, 1714, has: 'He learned the art of making Black Dogs, which are shillings, or other pieces of money made only of pewter, double washed ...' I can find no trace of this expression's survival in British urban slang.

Doit

A *doit* is a careless youngster up around Ballyclare in Co. Antrim. The *Ballymena Observer* of 1802 has the word, and defines it thus: 'A heedless youngster who would perhaps mismanage a message'. The word is from the Middle Dutch *dote*, folly, weakness of mind.

Dolsk

This Shelta word was collected by Master Green of Longford. It means a Protestant. *Dol* is a perversion of Irish *Gall*, a foreigner, also a Protestant, plus the arbitrary *sk*.

Donkey's gudge/Donkey's wedding cake

These two Cork city delicacies are not, I suppose, eaten in these relatively prosperous times, but Seán Beecher assured me that they were popular not long ago in poorer parts of the city. *Donkey's gudge* was, he said, 'a cake made from the remnants of the previous day's unsold cakes, with a layer of pastry on top and at bottom'. The *Donkey's wedding cake* had an addition: a layer of cream on top.

Gudge is interesting. As a verb it is found here and there in the dialects of England, and it means, according to the *English Dialect Dictionary* 'to stuff, eat ravenously or excessively. Hence *gudget*, a glutton'.

Dora

A Shelta word for bread, recorded by Master Green as *dora*. There are many recorded variants. *Dora gloch* is a baker; *shark a dora*, a slice of bread. Macalister suggests Irish *arán* as the origin, reversed and de-nasalised.

Doran's ass

Doran is a well-known family of Wexford Travellers, renowned for their knowledge of horses in the old days, and for playing the uileann pipes. It is not unusual for youthful Wexford go-boys to compare the size of their *membrum virile* to that of Doran's ass. I was shocked to the core of my being, gentle readers, to overhear a young one in a Wexford pub boasting recently that an acquaintance was hung like Doran's ass. Oh, the times we live in!

Dowdy

This is a noun I heard from the late John Vines, a rural philosopher who held court in a pub at The Willow Grove, near Delgany, in Co. Wicklow. The adjective is found everywhere, but the noun, as far as I can judge, may be heard only in parts of Dublin city and in Wicklow. It is found across the pond in Scotland and in England's North Country. It means an untidy woman, a streel. It is from the Middle English *doude*, a slut. 'Dido a dowdy, Cleopatra a gypsy', wrote Shakespeare in *Romeo and Juliet*.

Down the banks

This slang phrase for verbal abuse is quite common all over Ireland. I have no idea where its origin lies. Joyce has it in *Finnegans Wake*: 'My souls and by jings, should he work his jaw to give down the banks and hark from the tomb!'

Dry job

A slang phrase for an indoor job, such as a teacher's or a doctor's, considered comfortable by those who work out of doors. John McGahern uses it in *Amongst Women*: 'You mean a good dry job stretching into infinity with a pension at its end, is of no importance?'

Dublin cant from Ulysses

Joyce loved Dublin cant words. In *Ulysses* he has: 'Fumbally's lane that night; the tanyard smells.

White thy fambles *(hands)*, red thy gan *(mouth)*
And thy quarron *(body)* dainty is,
Couch a hogshead *(lie down and sleep)*
with me, then.
In the darkmans *(night)* clip *(embrace)* and kiss.'

All these cant words were imported from England. *Darkmans* (singular, you'll note) is, I think, a lovely word; it had a variant, *darky*, found in the late eighteenth-century Dublin song *The Night Afore Larry was Stretched.*

The quatrain quoted by Joyce, above, is from *The Rogue's Delight in his Strollinge Mort*, printed in Richard Head's *The Canting Academy* in 1673. I am indebted to Dr J.B. Lyons of the Royal College of Surgeons in Ireland for identifying the source of Joyce's quatrain for me, when so many Joyceans had failed. The suffix *mans*, by the way, comes from Latin *mens*, mind, through the ablative *mente*, 'with a mind, intention, mood', according to Partridge.

Dullamoo

I recorded this word in south-east Wexford. It means a wastrel. It is also a pejorative word for a homosexual man. A corruption of the Irish (*ag*) *dul amú*, going astray.

Dumnik

You shouldn't have any difficulty guessing the origin of this Shelta word for Sunday. It is, of course, the Irish *Domhnach*.

Dump

This is a verb used by schoolboys in Tuam. It means to evacuate the bowels. A context might be, 'An bhfuil cead agam dul amach? I want to go for a dump.' A likely scenario.

Duncher

This is a man's flat cap. Benedict Kiely has the word in *Drink to the Bird*: 'He wore a flat cloth cap, or duncher as they used to call it in Belfast, with a button on the top of it.' I have never heard the word used outside Ulster. Of uncertain origin.

Dust/Jotts

These are Tuam slang words for money.

Egg nog

Not what you think it is. To the pupils of Ballyrashane School in Co. Derry it meant 'eggs scrambled (no milk added) and fried in bacon fat in a pan'.

Faggot

A bad-tempered woman. I've heard the word in Dublin, Meath and Monaghan; perhaps it is much more common. Joyce used it in *Ulysses*. (See *Leg of*.)

Fardel

The late Liz Jeffries of Neamstown, Kilmore, Co. Wexford, gave me this word in the 1970s. It means a bundle of sticks, straw, hay, clothes, etc. 'All he had going to sea as a young fellow was a fardel of clean clothes,' she said to me, with reference to a neighbour. You'll find this word in many of the dialects of England, Scotland, the Isle of Man, and in the south-western counties of Cornwall, Dorset and Devon. From the Old French *fardel*, later *fardeau*, diminutive of *farde*, a burden.

Fay

Fay is the Shelta word for meat. *Sharogue fay* is raw meat. *Fay gawt* is veal. *Fay kleetug*, mutton. (Master Green gives *bleater's fay* for mutton.) *Blanogue fay* is beef; *mwogue's fay*, bacon. *Fay* is a deliberate distortion of Irish *feoil*, meat.

Feek/Tome feek

Feek in Tuam slang is both a noun and a verb. As a noun it means a girl; tome means special, lovely, so now you know how to chat up a Tuam girl. *Feek* is also a verb, and the *Beginner's Dictionary of Tuam Slang* says that it means 'to love one's partner with feeling'.

Figairy

This word is not confined to Ireland, as the *English Dialect Dictionary* would lead one to believe, but it is certainly much more commonly used here than across the water. A *figairy* is a whimsical notion or fancy; and I am pretty sure that it is a variant of the Standard *vagary*, from the Latin *vagari*, to wander.

Flake

A hill farmer in the Mourne mountains sent me this interesting word, which I've not come across in any other part of Ireland. This Co. Down *flake* is of Scots origin and it means a temporary gate to close a gap. I am inclined to believe that the word's ultimate origin was Old Norse *fleki*, defined in Vigfusson's dictionary as a hurdle.

Fleech

This is a verb you may hear in parts of Antrim and Down. It means to coax, cajole with a degree of flattery; to beseech. Henry Boyce from Cushendall sent me the word. The *Ballymena Observer* of 1892 has it as well. In the best Ulster Scots it gives: 'A fleeched at him tae A was tired.' This is a Scots word of Germanic ancestry. Compare the Modern German *flehen*, to beseech; and the Dutch *vleien*, to flatter. 'Duncan fleeched and Duncan prayed,' wrote Rhymer Rab in *Duncan Grey*.

Flibbertygibbet

This noun was common enough where I grew up on the banks of the Barrow. I had always thought the word to mean a ragged person, a tatterdemalion. Friends of mine from Kilkenny and Waterford confirmed my own definition, but when I went searching for the origin of the word I found that Oxford says it is an onomatopoeic representation of 'chatter', and holds that the earliest form of the word, *flibbergib*, is probably the original. *Flibbergib* also meant a flighty or frivolous woman.

Oxford quotes one of Latimer's sermons before Edward the Seventh in 1549: 'These flybbergybers an other dayes shall come and clawe you by the backe.' In 1611 Cotgrave's *French-English*

Dictionary defined 'coquette' as 'a pratling, a titifill, a flebergebit'.

The *English Dialect Dictionary* says that our *flibbertigibbet*, a ragamufin, is found only in Warwickshire, Berkshire and Somerset across the water. Where did we get our meaning, I wonder? Probably from the ragged, talkative urchin of Sir Walter Scott's *Kenilworth*, 'Dickie Sludge, or Flibbertigibbet', it has been suggested.

Funk/funky

First mentioned as Oxford University slang in *Junius' Etymologicum*, published in 1743, *funk* means a state of cowering fear, panic, or shrinking terror. It is still common in Ireland, especially among schoolboys. Oxford says that it may have come from the Flemish *fonck*. But there is another *funk*, a far more interesting word. You may hear it in parts of Kildare, Carlow and Wexford, and it is a word associated with foul smells. I can attest to the fact that in my schooldays *funk*, noun, was commonly used instead of *fart*. And *funky* to us meant smelly.

The first mention of this *funk* in literature was in W. King's *Furmetry*, written in 1699: 'What with strong smoke, and his stronger breath, He funks Basketia and her son to death.' Captain Grose in his *Dictionary of the Vulgar Tongue*, published in 1795, has a description of *funking the cobbler*, a schoolboy's prank: '... performed with assa faetida and cotton, which are stuffed into a pipe ... and the smoke is blown through the crannies of a cobbler's stall.' In the nineteenth-century the adjective *funky* appeared, to describe a person or place giving off a bad odour. Sometime in the 1950s American jazzmen began playfully applying the adjective to earthy, uncomplicated music that had, if I'm not mistaken, a bluesy tinge to it. The meaning was immediately extended to swinging, fashionable – quite a journey from its origin, the French dialect *funkier*, which came from Old French *funkier*, *fungier*, which came from Latin *fumigare*, from *fumus* smoke.

Gaaby/Gaby

The full forward at a football match I attended recently in Co. Wicklow fell in the square, as we used to call it before the GAA commentators started to show their erudition and call it a parallelogram. He immediately appealed for a penalty. He didn't get it, so he continued to sulk while sitting on his backside, and was told by an enthusiastic female follower of the opposing team to 'get up, you useless gaaby'. A *gaaby*, she kindly informed me, was a stupid fool, a blockhead.

I afterwards found the word in the dialect dictionaries under *gaby*, which has, it seems, a variety of pronunciations in Ireland, Scotland and the English midlands. Our own Jane Barlow, a writer I find interesting only for her use of dialect, has 'Entrusting so critical a task to a quare blundering gaby like Larry' in her *Irish Idylls*, published in 1892. Jane, I feel, would have pronounced the word *gaybe*; that's how I heard the word from a Sligo friend. Dickens, I note, has the word: 'Little Dorrit ... asked who it was, to which Fanny made the short answer, "that gaby."'

Some sources tentatively suggest that the word is associated with *gape*, which has its origin in Old Norse *gapa*, to open the mouth as the stereotypical fool is said to do. Others have suggested the Old Icelandic *gapi*, a rash, reckless person. Oxford, I see, tends to discount this latter theory.

Gabslick

This word for a chatterbox was collected by the pupils of Ballyrashane school, near Coleraine.

Gaff

This is a Dublin slang word for a home, a house. Origin unknown. Roddy Doyle has the word in *The Van*: 'If he'd been in his own gaff he wouldn't have been sitting like this, like a gobshite' (q.v.).

Game ball

This expression is sporting slang. It means in an excellent state. It's from the game of handball; the *game ball* is the final toss to a beaten opponent. So, people answer 'game ball!' to questions like, 'how are you feeling?'

Gangrel

A good word for a lout, usually one of no fixed abode and with no visible means of support, is *gangrel*, found in many places in Ulster.

This is an old word that has miraculously survived. Hampole speaks of 'gangrels and langeelers' in his *Perfect Living*, written sometime prior to 1340. Burns, in *Jolly Beggars*, has 'a merry core o' randie, gangrel bodies'. *Gangrel* is thought to be from *gang* on some obscure analogy, according to the *Oxford Dictionary*; the ending occurs, though perhaps from diverse sources, in several depreciative terms, as *haverel*, mongrel, wastrel. *Gang*, a set of things or persons, is Germanic in origin. For example, the German *gang* applied to a set of things – of cartwheels, horseshoes, etc.

Gansel

Not many words have escaped the net thrown by the *Concise Ulster Dictionary*. I was sent one such word some time ago. I had heard it myself many years ago from Mrs Mary Sweeney from Meenbanad in the Rosses of Donegal, who lived to be 104. Having failed to find it in any of the word lists compiled in the nineteenth century in Ulster, I thought that the old woman must have picked it up in Scotland, where she had to go to find employment long before she entered her teens. But now I hear from Mrs Mary Ross from Belfast that the word is heard in that western outpost of Scots, east Donegal and West Tyrone, the Laggan valley. The word is *gansel*, and it means garlic sauce.

Gansel, the old Scots dictionaries tell us, is *the* condiment to go with goose.

In Edward Kelly's *The Complete Proverbs of Scotland*, written in 1721, you'll find this: 'A good goose, but she was an ill gansel. Spoken when one has done a good turn, and by her behaviour after spoils the grace of it'.

The word is from the Old French *ganse*, a sauce, plus *aille*, a derivative of *ail*, garlic; in later French *janse d'aulx*, used in the same way. It was made in Donegal, as it was in the days of the fifteenth-century *Liber Cocorum*, from crushed garlic and milk.

Gates/gates wide

This is a Tuam adjective meaning very knowledgable. It is usually used with 'wide', as in

'He is gates wide about politics.' Or a young fella might be said to be 'gates wide about budgies' (q.v.).

Gattle

This is a Cork city slang for the youthful pastime of chasing girls. 'He spends his time gattlin' instead of sitting down with a book and thinking about his exams,' was how I heard the word used. Of unknown origin.

Gee

This is low slang for vagina. It has found its way into Irish literature. Samuel Beckett's *Dream of Fair to Middling Women* has: 'Lilly Neary has a lovely gee.' Roddy Doyle has the word as well in *The Van*: 'He'd had to keep feeling them up and down from her knees to her gee.' My friend the late Richard Wall, Joyce scholar, pointed out that Joyce used the word at least twelve times in *Finnegans Wake*, usually in puns such as 'Gee up, girly!' From the Hindi *ghí*, defined by Oxford as 'butter made from buffalo or cow's milk, clarified by boiling so as to resemble oil in consistency'. A Dublin word, brought home by the Fusiliers.

Gee/fanny gee

Gee is a Tuam noun for information. *Fanny gees* are lies, false information. One might set up a gomie (q.v.) with fanny gees.

Geeser/geezer

According to Eamon Mac Thomáis, authority on old Dublin life and customs, this was 'the nickname or slang word for a cat'. Of course the British *geezer*, an old codger, is also heard. This second *geezer* is from *guiser*, a mummer; hence any grotesque or queer character.

Get/git

A love child. Seán O'Casey in what I consider his best play, *Cock-a-Doodle Dandy*, has the lines: 'You one-eyed gett, if you had two, I'd cyclonise you with a box!' Richard Wall reminded us of Joyce's racy use of the word in *Ulysses*: 'The curse of a goodfornothing God light sideways on the bloody thicklugged sons of whores' gets!' The word is from *beget*, itself from Old Norse *geta*.

Getting

A Ballyrashane school word. In that part of Co. Derry *getting* means being attended to, or waited on. You'll hear 'Are youse getting?' from shop assistants and waitresses.

Gick

This is a Dublin slang word for excrement. As far as I'm aware, it is used mainly by schoolchildren to tease unfortunates who have been short taken. In *Paddy Doyle Ha Ha Ha* by Roddy Doyle there is 'IT'S ALL DOWN YOUR LEG – GICK GICK-LA-LA.' I haven't heard this word outside Dublin.

Gills

This *gills* is defined thus in the aforementioned Tuam *Beginner's Dictionary*: 'human being, used solely with possessive adjective, as in *My gills*, me, myself; *Your gills*, you, yourself.' I wonder is gills related to the *gill* referred to in Eric Partridge's *Dictionary of Historical Slang*, where it is defined as 'a fellow, a chap', considered low slang or cant by 1812? All we can do with most slang words is guess as to their origin.

Gipo

This is Dublin low slang for semen. I am indebted to Richard Wall for pointing out James Joyce's use of the word in *Finnegans Wake*: 'Gipoo, good oil.'

Glake

Many's the man made a glake of himself chasing women. I heard the word in Kilkenny, Wexford and Carlow. It means an eejit. Well, there's the Irish *gléic*, pronounced 'glake', a fool; but could this, I wonder, be related to the Scots and Ulster Scots *glaik*, a contemptuous epithet applied to a person? The *Concise Scots Dictionary* offers no etymology. The *Concise Ulster Dictionary* is not very helpful either.

Glassey alley/blood alley/blooder

These are words for certain types of marbles. They are Cork words, and the first of them was recorded by Seán Beecher. As a former marbles champion myself, I can record that they were unknown where I grew up in Co. Wexford. Eric Partridge has *glassey alley* from nineteenth-century England. It was a large variety, and very much prized. The *blood alley*, also known as a *blooder*, was a red marble to Cork children. Leslie Matson gave me these words. Do they exist nowadays? Do children play marbles any more? I don't think so.

Glick

This means clever, cunning. 'We all know about you, you glick fucker,' sang Dermot Healy in *The Bend For Home*. This is the Irish *glic*, cute, cunning.

Glimmers

These, according to my Tuam informants, are spectacles, or as they put it, 'sight enhancing objects worn on the nose'. Eric Partridge has *glims* and *glimmers* as early nineteenth-century low slang for the eyes; whence *glimmers*, a pair of spectacles, from about 1860.

Gloak

A look. 'I might as well go for a gloak, anyway.' Tuam slang.

Gloit

The *Ballymena Observer*, a treasury of Antrim words, published in 1892, has this word. It is also found in Scotland. It means a blockhead, a lubberly fellow, a lout. It comes from the Scots Gaelic *gloichd*, defined as a stupid blunderer, a half-wit, an idiot, in Malcolm Maclennan's dictionary.

Glouter

The pupils of Ballyrashane school, near Coleraine, gave us this word. They defined it as 'tapioca'. *The Concise Ulster Dictionary* has the word as 'a sticky mixture or mess'. The first syllable rhymes with 'how'. The word is Scots, origin unknown.

Glue

In such phrases as 'You have your glue.' Dublin slang for 'shit'.

Go-boy

A fairly common cant or slang term for a sly ruffian.

Go-by-the-wall

James Joyce was fond of this expression which describes a sly, sneaky person. In his *Portrait of the Artist As a Young Man* he has: 'Did you ever see such a go-by-the-wall?' He has it in *Finnegans Wake* as 'go be dee'. Another phrase of the kind is 'tickle-the-bricks' [q.v.].

Gobshite

This rude slang word is an English import that has found a permanent life in the speech of this isle of saints and scholars. In England it seems to be on the way out; indeed when Joseph Wright finished his monumental dialect dictionary around 1906 it was considered confined to the county Shakespeare grew up in, Warwickshire, and to Chester. It was often spelled *gawpshite* and *gaubshite*. It is hard to define. Wright's definition is 'a fool, a blockhead; an awkward, ill-kept, dirty person'. I think we in Ireland could add to that. At any rate, the second element in the word is from the unattested Old English *scita*, a word of Germanic origin; compare Old Norse *skital*, to defecate, and Middle Dutch *schitte*, excrement. The first element is related to dialect *gaby*, *gawby*, *gooby*, *gorby*, *goby*, etc., a simpleton, an eejit. These words are of unknown origin.

I am reminded of an atrocious pun that went the rounds in the days of the Kerryman jokes in the 1970s: Question: What would you call a Kerry Muslim? Answer: A gob-Shiite.

Going the two days

This is a Dublin slang expression known to James Joyce. It means behaving in a strange manner. In *Ulysses* he has 'Going the two days. Watch him! Out he goes again. One way of getting on in the world.' I have failed to find a reasonable explanation of the phrase. The eminent Joycean

Richard Wall told me not long before his tragically early death that he had also failed. He was a native of Ringsend, in Dublin.

Gomie

A noun from Tuam, this *gomie*. It means, a dolt, fool. It is from the Irish *gamall*, a fool, an eejit, or from *gom*, which is from English *gaum*, a simpleton.

Gongy

This is a Co. Wexford adjective meaning long, thin, ungainly. It is used only of men. One of the last of New Ross's coachbuilders was nicknamed 'Gongy' Pine. Séamus Moylan gives an unattested *gannga*, 'a fellow with long legs', from Co. Kilkenny.

Goolies

Dublin slang for testicles.

Goutrie/goutril

You'll find *goutrie* for a bad-mannered, careless, insensitive person in west Tyrone and east Donegal. The other noun, *goutril*, must be related; it is found in many parts of Ulster and it means a good-for-nothing, lazy lout. Both words may be forms of *gutter*, in its Scots sense, a stupid, messy workman, what would be called in parts of the south a *gobawn*, from *An Gobán Saor*, a mythical expert builder.

Grawg

This is Shelta for a street; also a town or village. *Mislín to the grág* is given by Master Green as Shelta for 'going to town'.

Grawnse

Never quite trusted by Travellers, *grawnshes*, strangers, are simply *stróinséirí* in disguise.

Grawrk

Shelta for a field. *Grawrk* is obviously a corruption of the Irish *páirc*, a field.

Greesh

This is Shelta for heart. *Gami greesh* means ill-will. *Mwilshas greesh*, which means my good heart, is a Shelta toast.

Grey

This is Shelta for tea, or as we say in rural Ireland, and as they did in the best circles in eighteenth-century England, *tay*. There is another Shelta *gré*.

It's a verb meaning to get up, to rise, to spring up. This is a corruption of the Irish verb *éirí*.

Greyd

This is hair in Shelta. From the Irish 'gruaig'.

Grey-ed

Shelta for a bridge. Obviously from the Irish *droichead*, bridge.

Greypul

This is what the Travellers call a church. It is the Irish *séipéal*, chapel, in disguise.

Greytis

Travellers, for their own reasons, have their own Shelta versions of Christian names. *Greytis* and *Nythus* are James; the first from Séamus, it is thought. *Greetus* is Peter; also *Yeetis*. *Grunles* is Annie. *Grooteen* is Winnie. *Gisaun* is John; from Seán. *Kerribad* is Margaret. *Libish* is Philip. *Mótas* is Thomas. *Rawb*, *Rawbeen* and *Sranee* are words for Mary. *Sartin* and *Shrortan* are words for Martin. *Sratrin* is Catherine. *Shrikel* and *Shrike* are words for Michael; also *Styeemon*. *Stofirt* and *Stofrick* stand for Patrick.

Gruagach

Gruagach is a term of contempt for a small, interfering pest of a man, in parts of east Galway, so Mary Gantley, who was born near Ballinasloe, told me. One of the best examples of this species, she said, was as bald as a baby's bottom, which struck her as strange, knowing that *gruagach* is an Irish word which means hairy.

Well, the gruagach is one of the many kinds of fairy men you'll find in the stories the old people told. He was a tiny hirsute being who was a good skin at heart. He was thought to help farmers at harvest time by protecting the grain from farmyard pests such as rats and mice. It was believed that he could be very mischievous at times. One should never, never thank him for his troubles by leaving out food and drink for him as he watched over things at night. To attempt to thank him meant trouble, and it was said that many a farmer found his crop of oats infested by vermin, and that many a farmer's wife found her eggs broken and her butter ruined because of an offering made in good faith to the little hairy fellow.

Don't think that the gruagach was to be found only in east Galway. In Ulster the gruagach is a female fairy. John Hewitt wrote: 'We were afraid/Of ghosts or gruagach for she filled the glen/With shadowy forms.' And John Montague,

I remember, wrote a poem called *The Gruagach*. This hairy being seems to be female in Ulster, and downright malevolent. I prefer the southern variety.

Guiner

A hurler who holds the hurl with his right hand below his left, as the orthodox golfer does. This grip is frowned upon by many aficionados. I have never heard the word outside Cork city. Seán Beecher has it. Origin unknown.

Gulpin

This word, now considered slang, hasn't, as far as I know, travelled south from Ulster. It is from the dialect *gulp*, the young of any animal in its softest and tenderest state; a word found in Scotland and in Northumberland, in Lincolnshire, East Anglia and Hampshire. Hence *gulpin* a young child, and, figuratively, a gullible man.

Gulp comes from the verb meaning to swallow, which has a relative in the Dutch *gulpen*, to guzzle. *Gulp* has been in English for a very long time; Langland has *y-gulpid* and *y-golped* in *Piers Plowman* in the fourteenth century. *Gulpin* is probably from the compound *gulp in*; young animals are good at doing this.

It came to mean a credulous person. In British navy circles in the nineteenth century, a gulpin was a marine. *Notes and Queries*, one of academia's most venerable journals, said in 1867 that 'a marine was called a gulpin by the sailors, that is a person who would swallow anything told to him'.

An Ulster *gulpin* is always male. In the course of a long association with Donegal I have never heard gulpin used of a grown woman.

Gurrier

People never tire of arguing about the etymology of this Dublin slang word. The usual explanation is that it was brought home by Irish soldiers who fought alongside the French in the Great War, and that *gurrier* is simply the Dublin pronunciation of the French *guerrier*. But this is nonsense. The French *guerrier*, if it ever existed in demotic French, was certainly not current since medieval times. I stand by my contention that the word is from the onomatopoeic slang word *gurr*, verb, to snarl or growl as a dog, also found as *gurrie*. From this we get *gurry*, a brawl; a loud, angry disputation; a dog-fight, so that a *gurrier* is a man who might be thought to indulge in rowdy behaviour.

Gutty

A common pejorative slang word for a hooligan. Probably from *gutter*.

Gyook

This is Mrs Wall's Shelta word for (a) an old man and (b) a beggarman. She also had the word *gyookra* for a beggarman. A distortion of the Irish *geocach*, a vagrant, cadger, parasite, in all probability.

Hawk

Even the great *Oxford Dictionary* insists that what William Shakespeare had in mind when he had Hamlet say that he knew a hawk from a handsaw, was that the Dane knew a hawk from its natural prey, the *heronshaw*, *hansa*, *harnser*, all dialect words for the grey heron. The only person I had ever heard casting a doubt on this was a Warwickshire friend of mine, who told me that *handsaw*, a word for the heron, had never been recorded in her, and Shakespeare's, county, a place whose dialect has been given the fine-tooth-comb treatment by lexicographers for obvious reasons.

Eoin Ó Cofaigh, architect and past president of the Royal Institute of his profession, wrote to me to say that he doesn't agree with the decision of the great dictionaries either. He is worth listening to.

A *hawk*, he points out, is a name for a plasterer's or mason's mortarboard, and the word is still in use in Britain and Ireland in the building trade. Shakespeare was talking a working-man's language: a countryman, who also knew the tradesmen of a great city, would have no difficulty in distinguishing between two of the most common of tradesmen's tools.

The problem here for Oxford (they have told me so) is the lexicographer's perennial one of dating words: how old is *hawk* meaning a plasterer's mortarboard? Well, it is quoted in a tract on building by a man named Moxon in 1700: 'Tools relating to plastering: A Hawke, made of wood about the bigness of a square Trencher, with a handle, whereon the Lime and hair being put, they take from it more or less as they please.'

Did Shakespeare know the word a century earlier? Of course he did. Tradesmen are the most conservative of people when it comes to words relating to their occupations; the word may have existed in their lexicon for centuries prior to Shakespeare's time without ever having been written down. To me, Mr Ó Cofaigh's gloss is perfectly plausible. I hope that Oxford will reconsider their judgement.

John Joe Smyth of Willow Grove, Delgany, a master carpenter, tells me that a *hawk* is also a slang term for a mason's labourer in places; the fellow who carries the hod. I wonder if this is where the verb *to hawk*, to carry anything about with labour, comes from?

A *hawk* is also a cataract on a Wexford horse's eye. The origin of all these hawks? A mystery, I'm afraid.

Headache

Headaches are common red poppies. I heard the word in Co. Carlow, where they were once regarded as particularly obnoxious by the women of south Leinster, 'the more so to unmarried young women, who have a horror of touching or being touched by them', according to the *English Dialect Dictionary*, which didn't tell us why this was so. The word is known in England. John Clare, in *The Shepherd's Calendar*, published in 1827 has: 'Corn-poppies that in crimson dwell./Called headaches from their sickly smell.'

Heth

This is an exclamation of surprise you'll hear in Ulster. *Heth* is simply a euphemism for *faith*. Often spelled *haith* in Scotland, Burns, in *Twa Dogs* has 'Haith lads, ye little ken about it.' W.H. Patterson has 'Heth no! Heth aye! Heth an' soul but ye won't!' in his glossary of 1890.

H.L.I./Higos/Higo Shites

I have this extraordinary expression from Seán Beecher. It was, he said, usually heard at soccer matches when dissatisfied customers heckled a player. The shout would go up: *H.L.I.!* Apparently it stood for Highland Light Infantry, a regiment of the British Army who were not very popular with the Munster Fusiliers; they were not, it was thought, famous for their bravery.

From the Highland Light Infantry was coined the phrase 'He has a touch of the Higos', meaning he is a coward; to have the Higo Shites denoted a high level of cowardice.

Hoger/hume

Two words collected by the pupils of Ballyrashane school, near Coleraine, Co. Derry. Both mean a bad smell. Hoger is from French *haut gout*, well seasoned. Hume is of unknown origin.

Hogger

Dublin slang for a derelict who, in days of the old hogsheads of Guinness, used to go about swilling the dregs of the barrels left outside the pubs on Dublin's quays. The term is still in use for a person who scrounges drink.

Hoity-toity/hoyden

A lady from Bruff, Co. Limerick, surprised me some few years ago by telling me that her grandmother used the phrase *hoity-toity*, which to most of us describes a person who assumes superiority, 'airs', huffiness, in quite a different way. I was surprised because once, and only once, had I heard my correspondent's unusual gloss on the word, and this also in Co. Limerick, near the village of Pallasgreen.

The usual definition of *hoity-toity*, the one given above, was what John Keats had in mind when he wrote, in *Cap and Bells*, 'See what hoity-toity airs she took.' But L'Estange, a witty observer of the social scene, complained in 1668 about 'the widows I observed Clanking and Jigging to every Tune they heard, and all upon the Hoyty-Toyty, like mad wenches of fifteen.' This is why I was surprised to find the expression used in Limerick exactly as L'Estrange used it, as an adjectival epithet applied to giddy, thoughtless young ones. A search through the dialect dictionaries of England showed that the Limerick meaning is found only in Northamptonshire nowadays.

As to origin, it seems that the expression is from *hoit*, a verb (the *toity* bit is merely a reduplication). *To hoit* means to engage in riotous and noisy mirth, according to Oxford. Beaumont and Fletcher,

Shakespeare's pals, have 'Hark my husband he's singing and hoiting', in *The Knight of the Burning Pestle*. But where does *hoit* come from? Probably from *hoyden*, a rude, ignorant man, a clown, a boor. This word is not found in English before Shakespeare's time, and even he doesn't have it. His contemporary Thomas Nashe is credited with introducing the word into literature. Milton used it: 'Shall I argue of conversation with this hoyd'n?'

And where does *hoyden* come from? Probably from a word found in both German and Dutch, *heide*, which means health.

Hooly and fair

From Co. Down I was sent this phrase by an old friend, Drew Hamilton, with whom I had many's the pint in Trinity College's Buttery in the old days. Drew and I share an interest in Robert Burns and he knows well what Burns meant by the word *hooly* in his poem to J. Smith, written in 1795: 'But still the mair I'm that way bent/Something cries Hooly.' The word means slowly, carefully, cautiously, gently, and it is often found in Scots literature in the phrase *hooly and fair*, which means slowly and gently.

I am delighted to hear that the phrase has reached our shores. My friend heard a farmer from the foot of the Mournes say it to his daughter at a pony show: 'Hooly an' fair now, lass. Take it nice and easy.'

This *hooly* is ancient. Hampole in his translation of the 39th Psalm (c.1330) has, 'My God cum not holy' for the Vulgate's *ne tardaveris*. Douglas in his 1513 *Eneados* has 'Huly and fair on the cost I swam.' Later this phrase became proverbial. Ray's 1678 *Proverbs* has 'Hulie and fair men rides far journeys;' and Kelly's *Scottish Proverbs* of 1721 has 'Hooly and fair goes far in a day.'

And the origin of this *hooly*? The Middle English *hóly*, itself a word of Norse origin. Vigfuson's Old Icelandic dictionary suggests the Old Norse adverb *hógliga*, gently, calmly; the old Vikings also had the adjective *hógligr*, easy, gentle.

Hoor/hure

These are two Irish variants of *whore*. The words are more often applied to men than to women. John B. Keane has 'Oh, a pure hoor of a man' in *The Bodhrán Makers*; Kavanagh has 'Isn't he the two ends of a hure?' in *Tarry Flynn*. The Old English was *hore*; the spelling *whore* did not become current until the sixteenth century.

Houghmagandie

This marvellous Scots slang for fornication has reached Ulster. Burns has it in *Holy Fair*: 'There's some are fou (full) o' love divine/And some are fou' o' brandy,/And monie jobs that day begin/May end in houghmagandie ...'

How are you blowin'?

I've never come across this outside Dublin's East Wall district, where I taught school for a short time in the late 1950s. It means 'How are you?' James Joyce has it in *Ulysses*: 'Who should I see dodging along Stoney Batter only Joe Hynes. "Lo, Joe", says I, "How are you blowing?"'

How's your father

This is a phrase in common use in Leinster, and perhaps elsewhere, for all I know. It denotes sexual shenanigans. 'He's out for a bit of how's your father.'

How's your granny for slack?

This phrase I heard used for the first time in Newtownmountkennedy, by Commander Joe Dunne, R.N., who kept a famous pub in the village. He assured me that it was an old Dublin expression, said as an opening gambit by a shy young fellow who has the intention of asking a girl for a date; an ice-breaker if you will. It is nowadays said to men who deny anything more than a platonic relationship with a woman: 'Oh, yeah, you haven't got any further than "how's your granny for slack?"; is that right?'

Hurry

A Co. Antrim friend of mine uses this noun which means a bit of a row. Not necessarily a violent row; a good tongue-lashing could be called *a hurry*. This is pure Scots. W.H. Patterson's glossary of Antrim and Down words (1880) tells us that a hurry 'is the name given to the Irish Rebellion of 1798'. The word is used of the Rebellion in Florence M. Wilson's celebration of Thomas Russell, 'The Man from God-knows-where', hanged in Downpatrick in 1803: 'In the time of the Hurry we had no lead/We all of us fought with the rest ...' Some hurry, come to think of it!

The Antrim people also call pressure of work a hurry.

Ire

Ire has many meanings, and male sexual arousal is one peculiar to Cork city, as far as I know. 'I have a touch of t'oul' ire' is a cornerboy's way of explaining this particular condition. Seán Beecher, *the* authority on Cork slang, told me that this meaning was not at all confined to the lower orders; he had, he said, his informants in Cork's yachting circles.

As to origin, I doubt if the word comes from 'scars, redness of the skin from wind, cold, friction etc., heat of the blood', one of Dinneen's glosses on the Irish word *oighear*, pronounced 'ire'. There is another *oighear*, found in the term *oighear chuimilte*, a file. Now this word, is, I think, adopted from the English dialect word *ire*, which means iron. It is found all over southern England and has come to mean you-know-what in the low English of a naval town in that region. Here, I think, is the source of the Cork *ire*.

Jacks

This Irish form of *jakes* is from French *Jacques*; both words were known in sixteenth-century England. Who Jacques was I have no idea. Professor Manfred Görlach, the distinguished German philologist, once gave me an amusing quotation from a tract written in 1596 by the courtier Harrington: 'There was a very tall and servicable gentleman, sometime Lieutenant of the ordinance, called *M. Jacques Wingfield*, who coming one day, either of business or of kindnesses to visit a great Ladie in the Court; the Ladie bad her Gentlewoman aske, which of the Wingfields it was; he told her Jacques Wingfield; the modest gentlewoman, that was not so much seene in the French to know that Jacques was but James in English, was so bashfoole, that to mend the matter (as she thought), she brought her Ladie word, not without blushing, that it was *M. Privie Wingfield*; at which I suppose the ladie then, I am sure the Gentleman after, as long as he lived, was wont to make a great sport.'

Jibbets

Where I grew up in Co. Wexford schoolboys used to threaten to make *jibbets* of one another: small pieces, morsels, 'mincemeat'. Patrick Kennedy, the respected nineteenth-century folklorist from Wexford, spelled the word *gibbets* in his engaging *Evenings in the Duffrey*. 'They'd have made gibbets of him only for Tommy Whitty.'

The word is found in Hampshire and Wiltshire, where the meaning is confined to describing torn, ragged clothing. From Wiltshire, Wright's *English Dialect Dictionary* has: 'You never did see such a slut! Her gownd a-hangin in dirty jibbets (rags) aal about her heels.'

As to origin, Wright asks us to compare the Old French *gibe*, a bundle, a pedlar's pack. Oxford doesn't have the word, but in its treatment of *gibbet*, a gallows, it mentions the Italian *giubetto*, *giubetta* diminutive of *giubba*, a cloak. Could this be the word's origin, I wonder?

Jigger

This is Shelta for a door. Collected by Master Green in the early 1930s. I can't even guess as to the word's origin.

Jigget

This is a verb you'll hear in places in Connacht, parts of Ulster and in the south-east of Ireland. I heard it in Sligo. It has various shades of meaning: to ride a horse at a jog trot; to shake, jog; to dandle a child; to gad about in a silly, frivolous manner. Jane Barlow, the Clontarf-born novelist who spent most of her life in Raheny, uses it in *Kerrigan's Quality*, set in the west and published in 1894: 'His car went jiggeting back empty to Ardnacreagh.' You may remember *jiggety-jog* in the nursery rhyme said to children being dandled on the knee: 'To market, to market to buy a fat hog,/Home again, home again, jiggety jog.'

In Wexford and in England's West Country *to jigget* means to gad about, and it is usually said of women with a distinctly depreciatory implication. And if that fine nineteenth-century novelist, Elizabeth Gaskell, didn't shake, rattle and roll, she knew all about a contemporary dance called *the jigget*, performed by working men and women and frowned upon by everybody else: 'I ha' learnt the way now,' says a character in *Mary Burton*, a story of life in Manchester, 'two jiggets and a shake.'

Jigget and the *jig* it came from, were thought to be ultimately from Old French *gigue*, a kind of fiddle. This word, it was said, gave modern French *gigue*, the dance and dance tune, but it did not. Modern *gigue* was adopted from English *jig*, an onomatopoeic word with both musical and sexual connotations.

Jingler

Tuam slang for a telephone. 'I was on the jingler with a tome feek.'

Jinny

An effeminate man, according to *Some Handlin'*, the glossary compiled by the children of Ballyrashane school, near Coleraine, Co. Derry.

Jole

A retired schoolmaster from Cashel, Co. Tipperary, John Derby, sent me the word *jole*, which means the neck of a bottle. My friend heard an old Tipperaryman advising a young woman in a pub not to put the jole of a bottle to her lips in case other lips had been sniffing around it in the pub's cellar, which might lead to a nasty dose of liver disease. The only *jole*, or *joll*, of that nature I've ever come across has been recorded in Scotland, Warwickshire, Suffolk and Kent; it seems to be a variation of the word *jowl*. *Jowl* is defined as the jaw, cheek, face; and *jole* is also used figuratively of the cheek or side of anything in the English of the places mentioned above. *Jowl* has a pedigree. It is from the Middle English *cholle*, also found as *choll* and *chol*.

There is another *jole*, sometimes *jowl*, and this I've come across only once in Ireland, in the parish of Horeswood, near Campile, in south Wexford. Old Maggie Whitty had a farm there when I was young, just across the road from the school in which my mother taught. Maggie had a huge earthenware tub, made in Staffordshire, which she called a *jole* and in it she mixed feed for her calves, hens and turkeys. The Staffordshire dictionaries say that this *jole* or *jowl* was used there for laundry purposes only. This word, too, has a pedigree. I take my cue from Cotgrave's *French-English Dictionary* of 1610: he gives *jalle* as 'tub'.

Joog/scrocky

These are words sent to me by two Dublin physicians, one practising in the west of the county; the other in Blackrock. Dr John Fleetwood of Carysfort, Blackrock, was told by a patient that she hadn't a joog in her. On enquiry she said that she felt very tired. Joog might be described as Dublin Irish, because it is simply an anglicised spelling of *diúg*, a drop.

Scrocky means flaky, Dr James Clarke of Rathcoole tells me; an eighty-year-old patient complained that he had scrocky skin.

Scrocky is from the Irish *scrothach*, a variant of *scrathach*, which means flaky, the great Kilkenny-born nineteenth-century scholar, John O'Donovan, pointed out. The noun is *scroth*, or *scraith*, scurf.

Kemp/kemping/camping

The verb *kemp* is now obsolete, I should think, because of the great changes that have overtaken the farmer's world in recent times. *To kemp* meant to strive for mastery, to compete; as far as I can tell it was used exclusively of farmer labourers. It used to be found throughout Ulster and as far south as Louth and Meath, and it was certainly imported from Scotland.

A nineteenth-century treasury of Scottish lore has this: 'It was common for the reapers, on the last day, to have a contention for superiority in quickness of dispatch, groups of three or four taking each a ridge, and striving which should soonest get to its termination. This was called a kemping.'

I found the word in the *Ballymena Observer* (1892), in Knox's *History of Down* (1870) and in a story by Seumus MacManus called *Phelim Ruadh*, published in *Pearson's Magazine* in 1900. MacManus, A Donegalman, wrote *camping* for *kemping*, and his workers were spadesmen: 'I wrought with Denis, as we spaded up the South Slope field, camping.'

Kemp is from Middle English *kempen*, related to Middle Dutch *kempen*, *kimpen*, and Old Norse *kempa*. 'There es no kynge undire Criste may kemp with hym one' is from *Le Morte Arthur* of about 1420.

Killinchy muffler/pickeering

Killinch is a place in Co. Down, and a *Killinchy muffler* is a hearty squeeze, designed, one expert on these matters tells me, to muffle the faint protests of a fellow's mot as he engages in *pickeering*, the art of making romantic overtures to a woman. I've heard the word *pickeering* in Co. Kilkenny. Also common in Co. Westmeath, I'm told. Séamas Ó Saothraí, a friend who lives in Greystones, gave me both these words. Origin? I've no idea, I'm afraid.

Kraudug

Shelta for a hen. I first heard the word *kraudug* from Mrs Wall, a relative of the famous pipers, the

Dorans of Wexford. Mrs Wall taught Shelta to her family and spoke it to them. A distortion of the Irish *cearc*, it has been suggested. Master Green has it as *cródóg*.

Lamp

This verb may be heard in Cork. It means to watch, to be on the look out for. 'He have nothin' on his mind only lampin' women.' It seems to be a fairly new word, so I am inclined to think that it came from the practice of 'lamping' rabbits, in which a strong light is shone on them as they graze at night, confusing them, and seemingly rooting them to the spot, making them an easy target for the hunter.

Langer

When I was going to a boarding school in west Cork, now closed down, thank God and Paddy Lindsay, a *langer* was a penis; so you can imagine the jokes when a German boxer called Rudi Langer won some championship or other. Much later I heard sniggers in Cork golf clubs, would you believe, when the golfing Langer first came on the scene. *Langer*, meaning an obnoxious person, is a figurative meaning.

I'm often asked where the word come from. I'm afraid I don't know. Perhaps it is made from *lang*, meaning long, plus the suffix *-er*. Austrians use *langer* when they describe a tall, gangly person behind his back.

Langers

To be langers means to be dead drunk in Cork. Origin unknown. Possibly connected with above.

Leg of (to have the)

This slang phrase means to be in good standing with; to have considerable influence with. Joyce, in *Ulysses* has: 'That old faggot [q.v.] Mrs O'Reardon that he thought he had a great leg of ...'

Levit

A heavy blow with the fist. I've heard this word in West Cork, but it is also known in the city. Possibly a corruption of *leviathan*, a word that has been used by English slang-makers to denote 'heavy' in a variety of senses. For example, a *levy* is a hard drinker, a heavy hitter; a *levvy dan* is a heavy gambler.

Lewd of yourself

Reverend Dan Lyons of the Salesian College, Pallaskenry, Co. Limerick, wrote to me enquiring about the word *lewd* which his mother used in the phrase *lewd of yourself*. Lewd to most of us means obscene, but to the old lady it meant ashamed.

This meaning was once common in Wexford, in Leitrim and in Longford. Patrick Kennedy, the nineteenth-century Wexford folklorist, has this in his *Fireside Stories*, published in 1870: 'And didn't the poor fellows look very lewd o' themselves.'

What an extraordinary history the word *lewd* has. The meaning unchaste, obscene, is a development of the original meaning of the word, and dates from Chaucer's time; in the prologue to *The Miller's Tale* he has: 'Læt be thy lewed dronken harlotrye.'

The origin of the word *lewd* in its many shades of meaning is the Old English *læwede*, a word now thought to be unconnected to the ecclesiastical Latin *laicus*, lay, although that's precisely what *læwede* means: 'not in holy orders, not clerical'. In 1380 Wyclif was writing of lay brothers, 'lewid freris' who said 'four and twenti pater nostris for matynes'.

Another development was the meaning unlearned, unlettered. A tract from around 1225 spoke of 'lewede men' who didn't understand Latin. Then it took on the meaning common, low, vulgar, belonging to the lower orders. Chaucer in *The Miller's Tale* has: 'Ye men shul been as lewed as gees.' It also had the meaning bad, worthless, which survived until Shakespeare's time.

My correspondent's meaning still survives in south-west England. I'm glad to know that it is hanging on for dear life in places here in Ireland.

Lift

Ulster verb meaning to arrest. I once heard that 'Five men were lifted last night in the Bogside' in a Radio Foyle broadcast.

Loof

This is an Ulster word for the palm of the hand. The late Peadar Ó Casaide sent me the word from Monaghan. It is also found further north. It is regarded by some as slang, but in fact it is a very respectable and very old dialect word. It was first seen in English literature in the fourteenth century and was popular with the great Scots writers from Henryson to Burns. The latter, in *Willie's Wife* has: 'Auld baudrons [cat] by the ingle sits/An' wi' her loof her face a washin' ...'

Its origin is the Old Norse *lófe*, related to Gothic *lófa* and Old High German *laffa*, the blade of an oar; also to the Old Slav (Polish and Russian) *lapa*, paw. Then there is the Irish *lapa*, paw.

Lum

I've heard this word in the north of Ireland for a chimney. A *lum sweep* is a chimney sweep. The word is of obscure etymology. It is possibly an application of Old French *lum*, light, from Latin *lumen*. But the resemblance to Welsh *llumon*, a chimney, is worth noting. Robert Burns used the word in *Halloween*: 'He bleezd owre her, an' she owre him/Till fuff! he started up the lum ...'

Lungeous/lungis

Not far from the town of Dungarvan in Co. Waterford I recently heard a strange word which I jotted down as *lunjous*. An old man of my acquaintance used it to describe a bad-tempered, quarrelsome, vindictive person. I had never previously heard the word in Ireland, but *The English Dialect Dictionary* has *lungeous, lungus, lunjus* and *lunjies* from various places north of Warwickshire, and from a few places in the southern shires. It adds 'awkward, clumsy, unmannerly, rough, violent in play' to the definition given above. It is also used as an intensive in places: 'It's lungeous cohd this mornin' wi' this here black east wind', was recorded in Lincolnshire.

If I'm correct the word has an extraordinary history. I think it's a variant of a word found in the literature of the Tudors, *lungis*, sometimes *lungeis*. Lyly in *Euphues* (1579) has: 'If tall (they term him) a lungeis, if short, a dwarf.' To Beaumont and Fletcher, *lungis* was a long, lazy galoot. The Citizen's Wife in *The Knight of the Burning Pestle* laments over Ralph the Apprentice after one of his attempts at how's your father [q.v.]: 'O, husband, here's Ralph again! – Stay, Ralph, again, let me speak with thee. How dost thou, Ralph? Art thou not shrewdly hurt? The foul great lungies laid unmercifully on thee: there's some sugar-candy for thee. Proceed; thou shalt have another bout with him.'

Lungis, Oxford says, is by way of Old French *longis*, from *Longinus*, the apocryphal name of the Roman centurion who thrust his spear into Our Lord's side; by popular etymology associated with the Latin *longus*, long.

The Waterford man's *lunjous* is surely the Tudor *lungis*, and if so it has the blessing of our greatest dictionary. A most interesting survival it is.

Marrow/morrow/Mismorrow/Mismarrow

Aidan O'Hara, singer and expert on the culture of the eastern provinces of Canada, has in his time sent me some very interesting Donegal words, many of them from the writings of Harry Percival Swan. The verb *mismorrow* is one of them. 'Don't mismorrow the papers' means don't mix them up. Mismorrow is also a noun, one of a pair that does not correspond, anything that is wrongly matched: a black in a team of bay horses, for example.

The Scots dialect poet Wallace, from Dumfries, has this in *The Schoolmaster*, written in 1899: 'O we're a' mismarrowed thegither,/O we're a' misfitted and wrang ...'

Morrow, noun and verb, from which *mismorrow* comes, is also well-known in the north of Ireland as well as in Scotland and in England south of the border as far as Chester. It is sometimes found as *marrow*. The noun means a match, equal; an exact counterpart or likeness, a facsimile. 'Mysell for speed had not my marrow,' boasted the poet Hogg, while John Clare, the Northumberland poet has 'a mon wha's marrow's hard to beat.'

Marrow can also mean a companion, partner; hence *marrowless*, companionless, solitary, unmarried. A children's rhyme from Chester goes: 'The robin and the wren/Are god's cock and hen;/The martin and the swallow are God's mate and marrow.'

Morrow, the verb, is defined in W.H. Patterson's glossary of Antrim and Down words (1880) as 'to lend men or horses to a neighbour and to receive a similar loan in return when needed'.

Mebs

Mebs are testicles. Figuratively used to describe a man one dislikes for any reason. I haven't heard the word used outside of Cork city and environs. Origin unknown.

Merl/mirl

Merl is a word found in eastern Wexford. I have also heard *mirl.* The word is used in phrases such as 'He hasn't a merl,' which means he hasn't a tosser, a penny to his name. I've heard this word as well in Co. Kilkenny, up the river Barrow near the village of Graiguenamanagh, and in the beautiful south Carlow hamlet of St Mullins. Séamus Moylan has the word in *The English of Kilkenny,* I see. Oxford glosses the word as 'token coin or counter'; it comes from the Old French *merel;* the modern French is *mereau.*

Mickey

Slang word for 'penis'. James Joyce has it in *Ulysses*: 'I'll put on my best shift and drawers let him have a good eyeful out of that to make his micky stand for him.'

Milder/melder

This is a verb common in New Ross when I was growing up there. It means to rain heavily. 'It's mildering out of the heavens,' I remember my grandmother saying.

This appears to have been originally a milling term. A *milder* or *melder*, as some people pronounced it, was the quantity of corn ground at one time. The word subsequently came to mean, figuratively, a strong flow, a rush, a deluge. From the noun came the verb. *Melder/milder* is from the Old Norse *meldr*, flour or corn in a mill, according to Vigfusson's great dictionary.

Mingi man

I have to thank Bernard Share for this rare example of Irish Army slang. It means an itinerant trader; and it comes from the Swahili *mingi*, an adjective meaning much, many. Writing in the Aer Lingus trade journal *Cara* in 1980 about south Lebanon, he has: 'We were to hear a lot about the Mingi men ... *Mingi men* began with the Irish contingent in the Congo, and the word has not only followed the Irish around but has gained international currency ... Mingi men sell everything they think a soldier might need – and a number of things he can probably do without.'

Mitching/mooching

Why the blazes do some Irish people say and write 'playing truant from school' when they mean *mitching*, an old word that was good enough for Shakespeare?

Mitching and *mooching* are common here and across the water. *Mooching* means to idle; it is from Norman French *mucher*, to hide, secrete, and it is obvious that its meaning has been expanded quite a bit, over the centuries, as has the meaning of *mitch*, which is from Old English *mycan*, to steal. I have a feeling that both words, whatever their immediate origins, probably have a common Germanic antecedent; consider the Old High German *muhhan*, to prey upon.

In many parts of rural England *mooch* and *moocher*, *mitch* and *mitcher* have for centuries been associated with blackberry picking. Schoolboys, of course, were apt to dodge classes to engage in this activity; nevertheless, Falstaff, when he said: 'Shall the blessed son of heaven prove a micher and eat blackberries?' was probably referring not to truancy but to a picker of the luscious fruit of the bramble.

Monetary slang

Decimalisation, and then the introduction of the euro, have made many of our slang words for the various coins obsolete. In *Finnegans Wake*, HCE is called abusively 'Tanner and a Make'; both these coins were sixpences. Joyce also has 'Two Makes a Wing' in the same work. *Wing*, a penny, was pure Dublin; the other words were imported English slang.

In *Ulysses* Joyce has 'two bar and a wing'. He also has 'Two bar entrance, soldiers half price.' In Dublin slang, a *bar* was a shilling; in England it was ten bob. Lexicographer Richard Wall suggests that *bar* came from the stroke placed after a number to indicate shillings, e.g. *10/-*

Joyce's early use of the word hits on the head the theory that the word *wing* came into being from the beautiful old penny piece which depicted a hen with her wings oustretched to protect her chicks. The pre-decimal currency was not introduced until 1928; the advisory committee chairman, incidentally, was W.B. Yeats.

Bob, a shilling, has survived the currency change as a general term for money. You'll still hear things like, 'He's worth a few bob.'

Another slang term which has survived in Dublin and elsewhere is one that O'Casey used in *Juno and the Paycock*: 'Not as much as a red rex, man.' *Red rex* is from the king's head on the English penny and ha'penny.

Kick was another term for a sixpence. Eric Partridge says that it was the name given to a seventeenth-century coin of that value. *Lop* was a Cork word for a penny; a *tack* was a Cork sixpence.

Money – Tuam slang words

Clod: a penny; *Corner*: 50 pence; *Lat*: £1; *Flem*, £5; *Brick*: £10; *Ton*: £100. *Dust* and *jotts* are words for money.

I have no information about what they call new currency in Tuam; but no doubt the Tuam schoolboys are busy working on fresh slang for that.

Mooching shoes

My friend Eddie O'Sullivan, a native of Mitchelstown, Co. Cork, gave me this compound, used by his late mother Nora. She had eleven children to bring up in a time that was more difficult than ours, and if ever she had to have recourse to a bank, she used to wear her *mooching shoes*, shoes that were not the best quality, to emphasise her need. She pulled through against the odds and reared a successful family. [See *mitching/mooching*.]

Mot

Dublin slang for a girlfriend. It started life in the brothels of Holland in the sixteenth century or even before that date, as Jules Manchon pointed out in *Le Slang* in 1923. The Middle Dutch for a prostitute was *mot*; *mot-huis* was a brothel. 'The first time I saw a Flaming Mot/Was at the sign of the Porter Pot,' wrote an anonymous poet in a song printed in London in 1773 which has the intriguing title *The New Fol de Rol Tit*. The lady was on the game. Francis Grose's *Classical Dictionary of the Vulgar Tongue* (1785) says that *mot* was cant for a whore. But Jon Bee's *Dictionary of Slang* (1823) says that *mot* means 'a young woman, desirable as a sweetheart' – the Dublin definition of *mot*. Likewise, the American *mot* was, according to *The Lady's Repository* of 1848, a book about American slang, 'any decent female, a mother, a sister, or wife'.

Many lexicographers follow Partridge in, mistakenly, in my view, suggesting that *mot* is a variant of *mort*, another old (sixteenth century or earlier) word for a criminal's woman. The great man also said that by 1930 *mot* was obsolete everywhere. He must never have been in Dublin.

Mouldy

This slang adjective may be heard all over Ireland. It means drunk. Joyce puns on the word in *Finnegans Wake*: 'Though he's mildew-stained he's mouldystoned ...' *Mould* is pronounced to rhyme with *foul*.

Mullock/mullocker/mullocking

To mullock means to do something in a slovenly way. Often used of hurlers and footballers who are unskilled, who try hard, but don't achieve very much due to their awkwardness. Hence *mullocker*, and *mullocking*. Common words all over Ireland; it is nineteenth-century British slang which also made its way to Australia. Origin unknown.

Mutton dummy

This is what a friend of mine who comes from Bangor in Co. Down calls a yachtsman's plimsoll type shoe.

Narling

A lady who teaches school in west Waterford wrote to me about a word she heard in the schoolyard. A little girl came complaining that another seven-year-old 'is always *narlin'* at me'. A good word, nowadays usually spelled *gnarling*, and it means, you'll have guessed by the sound of it, growling, snarling.

But my correspondent has a right to her spelling; this is how the word is found in the *Shyp of Folys* of c. 1509, in a passage which gives a clue to the word's imitative origin, an imitation of the snarling of a dog: 'Though all be well yet he none aunswere hath save the dogges letter, glowming with nar nar.'

Shakespeare, in *Richard the Second*, says that 'gnarling sorrow hath less power to bite'. His, and the Waterford child's word, are figurative meanings of the verb *gnarl*, to gnaw, bite at, nibble, a usage now found only in England's North Country and in Somerset in the south. There are relatives in the Teutonic languages. Consider the modern German *knurren*, to grumble, snarl; Swedish has *knorra* and Danish *knurre* with the same meaning; Middle Low German has *gnurren*, and Middle Dutch *gnerren*, to grunt; Old English has *gnyrran* and *gnyrende*, the latter rendering the Latin *stridens* in the *Saxon Leechdoms* of c. 1000. A long journey to a Waterford schoolyard, wasn't it?

Neb/Nebby

An Ulster word for the nose; occasionally the whole face. The Ballyrashane school children have it in their glossary, *Some Handlin'*. This is a humorous application of the word; its true meaning is a bird's beak or bill. That splendid Scot, Ramsay, in his 1727 *Proverbs*, has: 'Ye breed of Saughton swine, your neb's ne'er out of an ill turn.' *Nebby* in Ulster, Scotland and northern England, means cross-looking.

The origin of the word is the Old English *nebb*, a beak or bill.

Newance

This Ulster word was explained by Willie O'Kane from Dungannon as 'for once, unprecedented'. He gives the following gloss: 'He got up early this morning for newance.' The word is often used without the preposition: 'Jack's working well to-day. That's a newance.'

Nuks

This is a Cork city expression for money. A young fellow might ask his friend if he could borrow some nuks so as to bring his girlfriend to the pictures. The origin of this is the Shelta or Travellers' cant *nuk*, a penny.

Nurls

This is a Derry city word for chickenpox. It's probably a variant of *knarles*, itself from *knar*, a knot in wood.

Nyuck

An Ulster word for to steal. The pupils of Ballyrashane school, Co. Derry, gave us 'He'd nyuck the hole out of a flute.'

Parish priest

Dublin slang for a pint of stout. Kevin D. Kearns has it in his *Dublin Pub Life and Lore* (1997): 'A black pint of stout with its white collar is called "the parish priest".'

Parliamentary side of your arse, sit down on the

In *Ulysses* Joyce has 'Arrah, sit down on the parliamentary side of your arse for Christ's sake and don't be making a public exhibition of yourself.' Richard Wall explained the Dublin cant phrase as shut up; sit down and be quiet.

Parochial House

Dublin slang for the loo. In *At Swim-Two-Birds* Flann O'Brien has: 'Pardon my asking but where is the parochial house, the bathroom, you know?'

Pawny

This is another of Seán Beecher's words from Cork city. I have never heard it anywhere else. It means rain. The origin of *pawny* is uncertain. It may be *pani,* Hindi for water, a word brought home by the Munster Fusiliers; but there is also a word in

Shelta, the Travellers' cant, *pani* or *pawnee*, which also means water. This is thought to be a borrowing from Romani. Take your pick.

Peach

This Tuam adjective means 'grand, splendid, majestic, fine', according to the schoolboys who compiled the *Beginner's Dictionary*, already referred to.

Petty

This is an Ulster word. Once upon a time I was advised by a landlady in an Antrim village where my car had broken down that if wanted the petty in the course of the night, I'd find it out the back. *Petty* is an outside toilet. It's from the French *petit*, 'little', as being a little house. It probably came to Ulster from Scotland, which has a considerable number of French words in her vocabulary, due to ancient political friendship.

Piddle

The verb *piddle*, defined by Oxford as 'to work or act in a trifling, paltry, petty or insignificant way; to trifle, toy, dally' is now considered Dublin slang; that other verb, *piddle*, to pee, is related.

The ultimate origin of the verb is unknown. It came into prominence in England in Tudor times. In 1545, Roger Ascham addressed a man who never ceases 'piddelynge about your bowe and shaftes when they be well'. In 1594 Carew wrote disparagingly about men who 'piddle somewhat in the art of versifying'; Fletcher, the Tudor playwright, complained about a lady who had begun 'to piddle with Philosophie'.

Birds piddled in the seventeenth century: in other words they scooped for food, and in the most unlikely places. The religious writer Barckley, writing in 1631, said of the prophet Mahomet: 'As he was preaching there cometh a dove flying towards him, and alighteth upon his shoulder, and pidleth in his eare for meat.' This meaning is now obsolete. In the same era, *piddle* began to mean to toy with food. In one of his sermons, a divine named Dyke spoke of 'disease that makes them eat nothing at all, or else they doe but piddle and trifle'. Byron, in *Don Juan*, refers to 'entrements to piddle with ...' This *piddle* is still heard in the English of Co. Wexford.

Now as to the other *piddle*, to pee, it still is with us in Ireland as well as in Britain. Captain Grose was the first to record it. In his 1790 *History of the Vulgar Tongue* he has: 'To piddle, to make water, a childish expression'. Sir Walter Scott used the verb figuratively, and to great effect, in a letter written in 1814. About a bad play he had seen, he says: 'The last act is ill-conceived. He piddles, so to speak, through a cullender and divides the whole horror of the catastrophe into a kind of drippety-droppets of four or five scenes.'

Pigeon

A lady from Athlone once wrote to me complaining that a total stranger in a midland hotel referred to her eighteen-year-old daughter as her young pigeon. Both mother and daughter found the term offensive. Fair enough.

Pigeon, for a young one, is quite common in Irish dialects and is also found extensively in Britain and in the United States. James Joyce used the word as a term of endearment in *A Portrait of the Artist as a Young Man*: 'Is that you, pigeon?' But the word was used of a woman back in Elizabethan times. Green, writing in 1592 about the thankless people often encountered in this imperfect world, wrote: 'When they had spent upon her what they had, then, forsooth, she and her young pigeon (her daughter) turne them out of doores like prodigal children.'

There are only a few references in literature prior to that, but we may be sure that good-looking women were called pigeons since the Middle Ages, when English borrowed *pyjon* from

Old French *pyjoun*, a dove, a young bird. The French word came from the Late Latin *pipio*, a young bird, from Latin *pipere*, to cheep, chirp. An imitative word this *pipere*, like the Greek *pipos*, a fledgeling, and long, long ago, the Sanskrit *pippaka*, a species of bird whose name was an imitation of its call.

Pineapple

Tuam slang for a church.

Plámás

This word is common in English all over southern Ireland. It means the white mouth, flattery. It is not a native word, however, and it made a fairly late entry into Irish literature. T.F. O'Rahilly suggested that Eoghan Rua Ó Súilleabháin (fl. 1780), a dab hand at the *plámás* himself by all accounts, was the first Irish writer to use the word. But it was in Irish earlier as *blámás*, attested to in Plunkett's dictionary of 1662. Its origin was *blancmange*, which came into English from Old French in the fourteenth century as *blanc-manger*, white food or dish, from *blanc*, white and *manger* to eat. It was concocted from fowl, minced with cream, rice, almonds, sugar and eggs.

Edmund Burke used the word figuratively for what Eoghan Rua called plámás, 'Whenever that politic prince made any of his flattering speeches ... when he served them with this, and the rest of the blanc-mange, of which he was sufficiently liberal ...'

Ponney

A ponney is a tin mug or cup, sold in my young days by tinkers. The word is in Seán Beecher's *Dictionary of Cork Slang* but the word was by no means confined to that city. It was, Mr Beecher said, 'used extensively in Cork schools when free milk was distributed to pupils'. I can find no trace of the word in dictionaries of British slang, and its origin is unknown.

Pony

This was a whiskey glass of stout, used as a chaser by those real whiskey drinkers who couldn't stomach a full pint or even a half pint of the black brew. A Dublin slang expression.

Pony up

Dublin slang for 'pay up'. James Joyce used the expression in *Dubliners*.

Pooley

This is a Cork noun for pee. Micheál MacLiammoir, the actor, used to tell a story that showed the sharpness of the Cork city audiences in the old Opera House. He and his partner Hilton played *Othello* there when things weren't too good financially, and a kind, but highly-strung English actress of note joined the company and played Desdemona for half-nothing to help them out. Edwards was Othello, and MacLiammoir Iago. All went well until Desdemona, near the play's end, decided to comb her locks, and to preen in silence for that little bit too long; a voice came from the audience when she stretched out on her bed at long last: 'Hi, Desdemona girl, you forgot to make your pooley.' The ensuing hilarity among the groundlings ruined the play. The actress refused every enticement to play the following night.

Poshteen

A man from Ballinteer in south Dublin gave me a very interesting word used by his grandfather, who lived in north Tipperary back in the 1950s. The old man used to call his sheepskin coat his *poshteen*. Who'd blame his grandson for thinking that the word was from Irish! But no. As he explained it to me, 'Much to my surprise I saw a picture in one of the papers of a member of the Taliban wearing what was described by the reporter as a *poshteen*. My grandfather was an old soldier who served abroad with the British Army. I take it that *poshteen* is an Afghan word.'

It is indeed, an erroneous form of *posteen*, an Afghan leather pelisse, generally made of sheepskin with the fleece on. Kipling makes reference to it in *A Day's Work*, written in 1898: 'William, wrapped in a poshteen, a silk-embroidered sheepskin jacket trimmed with rough astrakhan ...'

The Afghan word is from the Persian *postín*, from *póst*, skin, hide.

Power will have another day

I have heard it said that Eamon de Valera, when he was elected President, asked the political correspondents of the national newspapers to a party in Áras an Uachtaráin, at which a small libation of John Power whiskey was poured for the guests before the Chief said a few words of thanks. When he had finished speaking a butler reached for the bottle to replenish the glasses of the guests, but the austere Dev waved him away, saying, *Beidh lá eile ag an bPaorach*, or, as it's now in the English of Co. Waterford, *Power will have another day*. A good pun, don't you think?

I am often asked about the origin of the saying. Powers are as plentiful in Waterford as Butlers are in Kilkenny and as Ryans are in Tipperary; so who was the Power of the saying?

It is difficult to be sure about these matters, but the town of Dungarvan claims him as one of their own. His name was Edmund Power and I've read that he uttered the defiant words *Beidh lá eile ag an bPaorach!* as he stood on the scaffold to pay for his misdeeds, either as a 1798 man or as a Whiteboy hooligan, nobody seems to be certain which. He couldn't have been talking about himself, so what could he have meant? By *Paorach* he meant Waterford people; Waterford was *dúthaigh Paorach*, the territory of the Powers, as the late Donal Foley of *The Irish Times* once reminded me.

Prune

Dublin slang for a testicle.

Quim

This northern adjective is *not* related to the pretty, but obscene, term for the vagina. It is an adjective which means affectedly pleasant; moving with ease and precision; prim. The word was first recorded by William Lutton in *Montiaghisms*, published in Armagh in 1923. It is still to be heard along the banks of Lough Neagh, I'm reliably informed. It is an altered form of the Scots *queem*, smoothly, pleasant, from Old English *cweman*, to please.

Racker

This interesting slang word is found only in the territory hunted by the Ward Union Staghounds.

It means a man who opens gates and closes them again for members who might find themselves in some distress. *Racker* is interesting because it can be traced to the days of King William of the Boyne fame. Dr Brigitte van Ryckeghem, a scholar of Hiberno-English, tells me that in Holland it meant 'a commoner who assisted the landed gentry during hunts; a horseboy, also a ruffian'.

Rag

I heard this interesting word from an old Waterford fisherman. It means a sea fog or a drizzling mist. I see that the word is known in Devon, Lancashire and Yorkshire. It's of Scandinavian origin it seems; the Danish *rag* means a sea-vapour, according to the *English Dialect Dictionary*.

Rantan, on the/On the tear *(pr. tare)*

Both those slang expressions mean to be on a drunken spree. They were imported from England.

Rap, not worth a

This means 'it's of little or no value.' The rap was originally a counterfeit coin used in the eighteenth century when there was a copper shortage. Swift, in *Drapier's Letters* (1724), has: 'It has been many years since copper halfpence or farthings were last coined in this kingdom ... many counterfeits passed about under the name of raps.'

Rat (in a)

In parts of Co. Galway to be *in a rat* means to be in a bad temper. I heard the expression as well from my friend the late Pádraic Collins, a diplomat with a passion for words, born and reared in Fenore, in north Clare.

Rat-arsed

A Dublin slang expression for extremely drunk.

Reck

Reck in Cork means recognition. 'I didn't reck him,' means I didn't recognise him. Beecher in his Cork glossary also has: 'He didn't give him a reck.' The word is Germanic in origin. Old English has *reccan*.

Reek

Derry city slang for a smoke. To have a wee reek of a fag means to have a furtive smoke, Seamus Mac Connell tells me.

Riddle

This is a Tuam word for a toilet. Probably confined to schoolboys.

Rig

Tom Carr has sent me many interesting words connected with fishing over the years. He often heard *rig* for a fierce gust of wind, used by trawlermen.

This surely comes from the Old Norse *hregg*, storm and rain. A Wexford skipper told me recently that a lot of the old words connected with his business are dying out, supplanted by words adopted from modern technology. What a great pity this is.

Rippet

A *rippet* is a noisy disturbance, an uproar, a quarrel. I was sent the word from a man from Ballyclare, Co. Antrim.

The nineteenth-century glossaries of Ulster English have the word from Down and Antrim. The contemporary *Concise Ulster Dictionary* has the word as well, and with the secondary meaning, 'a romp, a frolic'. It is thought that the word is imitative in origin, and you may be sure that it came into Ulster from Scots. It's an old word. Dunbar, in *Tua Mariit Wemen* (1508 or thereabouts) has: 'He ralis, and makis repet with ryatus wordis.' Apparently the word made its way with the Ulster colonists in America in the eighteenth century, and that it is to be heard in places all along the east coast from Maine to Maryland. The word is Germanic in origin. Compare Frisian *rippe*, to tear, rip, and Flemish *rippen*, to rip, strip off roughly.

Rodney

This pejorative word I've heard in south Ulster counties and in Kildare and Carlow. A twit would be as good a way as any to define the word; a Kildareman I know told me that a Rodney was 'an insufferable little shite'. Richard Wall explained that Rodney is a common name for an English upper-class male in Irish jokes; he was generally considered effete. Patrick Kavanagh to my certain knowledge used the word a lot, especially when referring to bank managers. In his novel *Tarry Flynn*, he has: 'I thought it might be this rodney of an uncle of yours.'

Rosiner

Dublin slang for a stiff drink, often the first of a session, or as Beckett has it in *Murphy*: 'Reader, a rosiner is a drop of the hard.' Generally thought to be from the fiddler's practice of rosining his bow before starting to play.

Rossie

This is Dublin slang for a brazen hussy. It's from the Irish *rásaí*, defined by Ó Dónaill's dictionary as (a) a race; (b) a gadabout. Joyce has the word in *Ulysses*: 'If they could run like rossies she could sit so she said ...'

Sauch

My late wife, a Donegal woman, used *sauch* for a sally or willow. Sometimes spelled *saugh*, it's a Scots word; 'Naw whip nor spur but just a wattle/O' saugh or hazel,' wrote Burns in *The Farmer's Salutation.* It has given the adjective *sauchie* or *saughy*, abounding in willows, and there are interesting compounds. For instance a *sauch creel* in Donegal is one made from willows; a *sauch beck* in Cumbria is a stream with willows growing along its bank.

The origin of the word is Old English *salh* (Anglian), equivalent to West Saxon *sealh*, sally.

Scad-the-beggars

These are leeks fried in a pan, according to *Some Handlin'*, the glossary collected by the pupils of Ballyrashane school, Co. Derry.

Scar/scaur/scare

Donegal and Fermanagh people often use these two words instead of *scare*. Although *scar* is used in many English dialects from the North Country to Hampshire, the only places I've come across *scaur* are in remote parts of western and southern Scotland, and in Antrim and Down.

Scott used *scaur* in *Rob Roy*: 'It wad hae ta'en a hantle o' them to scaur Andrew Fairservice.' Both *scar* and *scaur* are used as nouns also. I heard 'I never got sic a scar in all me life,' from a woman in Creeslough, Co. Donegal.

The Middle English *skerre* normally became *skarre*; the form *scar*, now dialectal, is therefore regular. The Middle English word is adopted from the Old Norse word *skiarr*, whence *skirra*, to scare.

These northern words remind me of a southern horse-coper's adjective *scare*, which means easily frightened, cowardly. I've heard my friend Miley Connors, a Wexford traveller and horse dealer, use it. It comes from the Old Norse *skjarr*, shy, timid, Vigfusson, the great authority on these matters, tells me.

Screenge

This is an Ulster verb meaning to search carefully or frantically; to rummage. Seumus MacManus of

Donegal has it in his story *The Rocky Road to Dublin*: 'For books the boy screenged the countryside.' It seems to be a Scots form of the verb *scringe*, which, along with the above glosses, is also defined by the *Concise Ulster Dialect* as 'a lash, a blow with a whip or tawse, from the idea of lashing the water with a net'.

Screw

Dublin (and English) slang for an income, wages. James Joyce uses the word in *Dubliners*: 'She knew he had a good screw for one thing and he suspected she had a bit of stuff put by.' There is another slang screw: I heard it recently in Cork city. It means a bottle of wine. This is an old slang word; Barrington has it in his *Sketches* (1827-32): 'He was the hardest-goer at kettle or screw ... of the whole grand jury.'

Scruting

This is a word sent to me recently by a Wexfordman, who found it in a book by the well-loved folklorist and fiction writer, Patrick Kennedy. My correspondent quoted the context. It's from the charming *Fireside Stories*, published in 1870: 'If ever his princess and himself had a *scruting*, I know who got the upper hand.' It means, of course, an argument. The *English Dialect Dictionary* has the word from Wexford, but from nowhere else, and it can offer no clue as to origin. Neither can I, I am sorry to say.

Scunder/Scunner

Conrad Hennessy, an old friend of mine who now lives in Dalkey, asked me about the northern word *scunder*, which as a verb has a variety of related meanings. First of all it means to feel disgust; it also means to nauseate somebody; used loosely it means to annoy; and used with *at* it means to regard with disgust. The noun *scunder* means disgust, dislike; and something that causes disgust. You'll hear *scundersome* for repulsive; and to be *scundered* means that one is sick and tired of a certain diet. The very common *to take a scunder* at something or somebody means to develop an aversion to it or them.

The *Concise Ulster Dictionary* points out that *scunder* is a mistakenly 'corrected' form of *scunner*, a more common word in Donegal at least.

This *scunner* is found in Scotland and in North Country as well. Dunbar, in one of his poems composed shortly after 1500 has: 'In harte he tuke ... sic ane scunner.' Sir Walter Scott in *The Surgeon's Daughter* (1827) has: 'I thought she seemed to gie a scunner at the eggs and bacon that Nurse Simson spoke about to her.'

As to origin, nobody has a clue where these words came from. Oxford doesn't have *scunder* and as to *scunner*, it just says that it is a Scots and northern word.

Scurravogue

One of my valued correspondents is R.S. Boyd of Bangor, who has sent me many's the interesting Co. Down words. *Scurravogue* was a word of his father's, who was an Antrim man. Whenever young R.S. got up to some mischief, his father would use this mildly reproachful word, something akin to rogue or rascal.

From the sound of it I thought it might be from the Scots Gaelic, but no. It is undoubtedly from the Scots *scurryvaig*, glossed in Mairi Robinson's *Concise Scots Dictionary* as a vagabond; an idle, unkempt or slatternly person; a lout; a scullion. Nobody has traced it further back than Scots, although the Latin *scurra vagus*, a wandering clown, has been suggested. That, I think, is a long shot.

Scurrock

My first acquaintance with this rare word in Ireland came through the good offices of William T. Lyons of Aghamore, Ballyhaunis, Co. Mayo. It was, he said, one of his mother's words. When her offspring tried to cadge money from the poor woman, she would reply: No! Not even a *scurrock*.' Mr Lyons found the word in a Worcestershire dictionary, where it was glossed as a small piece; a shovel; an evil spirit. Well, since the good woman was certainly not referring to shovels or evil spirits, her son asked me to find out a little more about her *scurrock*.

It has turned up in Leitrim, Sligo, Roscommon and south Donegal. It is also found from Shetland to Scotland and northern England; and it has also gained a foothold in East Anglia and in Devon and Somerset as well. Oxford says that it may be related to *skerrick* and to *scuddick*, which have the same meaning, and concludes that all three dialect words may be slang in origin. I can find no mention of Ireland in any of the great dialect dictionaries in connection with the word, which is why Mr Lyons's recording of the word is quite important.

Scut/scutting

A pejorative West Waterford word for a flighty young person of either sex. *Scutting* means romping, staying out late at night and the like. A *scut* may get a bad name, but is generally harmless enough.

Segotia/St Fairy Anne

Me segotia, or *me oul' segotia* are phrases as Dublin as they come. I have come to the conclusion that Mr Paddy O'Neill, a schoolmaster from Lusk, who included it in a word list sent to me years ago by Mr Paddy Weston from the same part of north Co. Dublin, was right when he glossed it as a Dublin Fusilier's word. *Me segotia*, Mr O'Neill claimed, was originally said to children only, which is very important, as it confirms his theory that it was a corruption of some phrase like *mon cher gosse*, my dear child. If you think that's a bit far-fetched consider other phrases in which the returning soldiers made a hames of French: they gave us *Saint Fairy Anne* for *cela ne fait rien*, for example, used when they meant 'it doesn't matter' or 'don't worry about it.'

Shade

A Traveller's word for a policeman, recorded by Master Green. Perhaps this is from the English slang verb *shade*, to shadow.

Sham

Tuam slang for an upright gentleman.

Sharagy

Shelta for a soldier. Master Green collected this word in Longford. Mrs Annie Wall gave it to me in Co. Wicklow. See *Sharogue* and one may deduce that Sharagy is derived from the 'red coats'.

Sharogue/sharogue fay

This means red, or red-haired, in Shelta. *Sharogue fay* [q.v.] is raw meat. *Sharogue* is thought to be a distortion of Irish *dearg*, red.

Sharpogue

This is Shelta for a boy. MacAlister says that it is a distortion of Irish *gasúr*, boy.

Shed a tear for Ireland/Parnell

The slang phrase to shed a tear for Ireland, means to have a pee. I heard it in Dungarvan from Eddie O'Sullivan. Richard Wall gave me *Shed a tear for Parnell.* He quoted Eamon Kelly and his *English That For me and Your Humble Servant*: 'When he came in after shedding the tear for Parnell, he lifted up the cradle and put it back on the floor.'

Shrach

A Shelta word for a tree. A perversion of the Irish *sceach*, a bush, especially a whitethorn bush. Wexford Traveller Miley Connors gave me the word.

Shteema

Mrs Annie Wall's Shelta word for a pipe. Either from English *steamer* or a perversion of Irish *píopa*, pipe.

Shuggly-shoe

This is a word I heard in Dunlewey, at the foot of Errigal. It's a child's word for a see-saw. Isn't it nice! I note that William Lutton in his *Montiaghisms* (1923), a glossary from the banks of Lough Neagh, gives the following definition: 'A suspended rope in which children swing one another for amusement'.

Skai/skaihope/Skaihope groot

Skai is Shelta for both water and the sea. From the Irish *uisce,* water. Wexford Traveller Miley Connors gave me the word *skaihope* for whiskey. A distortion of the Irish *uisce beatha,* water of life. Old Mrs Wall, also from Co. Wexford, gave me the term *skaihope groola* for cider. *Grool* is the Shelta word for 'apple', from the Irish *úll. Skai-groot* is Miley Connors' Shelta expression for America. *Groot* is Shelta for 'new'.

Skate

This is Tuam slang for a dance and a dancer. Also used as a verb.

Skelm/skellum

This is none other that Robert Burns's *skellum*, a word for a scamp, rascal, scoundrel, that has also survived in Scotland and in England's North Country. But the word, in the form *skelm*, is still used in places near Cullybackey in Antrim, and it also hides itself in a few places in the footholds of the Mourne mountains in Co. Down. You'll remember that passage in Burns's great *Tam O'Shanter*: 'She tauld thee weel thou wast a skellum,/A bletherin', blusterin', drunken blellum.'

Ben Jonson had the word long before Burns's time. In 1611, in *Coryat's Crudities, Introductory Verses*, he wrote: 'Going to steal 'em/He findeth soure graspes and gripes from a Dutch skelum.' And that oul' skellum, Pepys, told his diary on the third of April 1663 that an acquaintance 'ripped up Hugh Peters, calling him "the execrable skellum".'

The word is a Dutch emigrant. The Dutch *schelm* is from the German *schelm*, rascal, devil, pestilence, carcass, etc. The Middle High German is *schelme*, and the Old Norse *skelmir*.

Slaister/sloister

The verb *sloister* was sent to me by a Belfast friend of mine, Jane Ross, who heard in up in the Glens. I myself have heard *slaister* at the back of Muckish in Donegal. The verb means to be engaged in wet, dirty work; also to bedaub, spatter, plaster; to make a wet, dirty mess. In Donegal I heard a mother telling off her young daughter who was preparing to go to a dance, for *slaistering* her face; the young one was applying too much make-up, her ma thought. I've also heard the verb used of a man walking through mud, 'slaisterin' his way home.

Slaister is also found in Scotland, and in the northern counties of England in all of the senses I've mentioned above. *Slaistrel*, a messy worker, is a fine Northumberland derivitave.

What good words beginning with *sl-* we have for messy, mucky things: *slobber*, *slob*, *slubber*, *slime*, *sludge*, *slop*, *slush*, *slotter*, and the medieval *slutterbugges*, dirty people, come to mind. The origins of these can be traced, but I have no idea where that fine word *slaister* comes from, I'm sorry to say.

Slammick

A slammick is an untidy, awkward woman. I heard the word many times in west Cork, where you'll also hear *slaimice*, the Gaelic version. The word is from English *slammock*, which the *English Dialect Dictionary* defines as 'a dirty, ungainly person; a slattern'. It also has the word *slammockin*, 'a dirty, slovenly woman'.

Slang or cant in Dublin songs from the 1780s

The Irish scribe Muiris Ó Gormáin preserved some songs from the Dublin of Grattan and Burke; they are to be found in MS G 482 in the care of the National Library of Ireland. 'They were', he assures us, 'quite the Ton with the inhabitants of Dublin in 1788.' One of them is *The Night Afore Larry was Stretched* (hanged).

Larry was really Frederick Lambert, hanged for murder in the year mentioned by our scribe. Here are some of the slang words from this great song, which has been recorded by the Dublin folk singer Frank Harte:

Bait was the food they brought Larry before he was **stretched**, hanged. Nine **glims** that were lit in his cell were lanterns, not candles. The **trap-case** was the condemned cell; **case** was a house; **daddle**

means hand; **Claret**, blood. The **nubbling chit** was the gallows; *nubbling* was hanging; *chit* was a variant of English cant *cheat*, *chet*, meaning 'thing'. **Darky** was 'night' (see *darkman*). **To take a ground sweat** meant to be buried.

Another execution song is *Luke Caffrey's Kilmainham Minit.* Kilmainham was Dublin's Tyburn, and the **minit** was not the length of time it took the poor Mr McCaffrey to die on the scaffold, but refers to his macabre dance at the end of the rope. The song is about the failed attempts of his friends to revive him by injecting whiskey into his jugular.

Slops

I am reliably informed that *slops* are no longer worn by Dublin schoolgirls. The word is remembered by girls who had to wear them, though. Out of fashion nowadays, they were, it seems, highly recommended by the nuns in days of yore. There were knickers with long, loose legs that descended to the knee. Better for a young fellow to see the legs of the slops than a glimpse of real flesh, so the argument went.

Slops (always plural) were known to Shakespeare. In *Much Ado About Nothing*, Don Pedro makes reference to 'a German from the waist downward, all slops.' Of course *slops* in this instance meant loose garment of any kind, including trousers. You may remember Mercutio's salutation: 'Signior Romeo, bon jour! There's a French salutation to your French slops.'

Slops are probably related to Middle Dutch *slop*, a long, loose, garment, and to Old Icelandic *sloppr*.

Snash

I once heard a mother say, as she reprimanded her young son for acting the maggot, 'I don't want any more snash from you.' Robert Burns has this word, now regarded as slang, in *Twa Dogs*: 'How they maun thole a factor's snash.' The word is found all over the north of this country. Seumus MacManus from Donegal has it in his 1895 novel, *The Bend of the Road*: 'I doubt if they'll put up with your snash elsewhere.'

An imitative word, this, I think; but some say that it may have Scandinavian connections. Compare the West Frisian *snasje* and the Swedish *snaska*, in the sense to bite at, hastily and noisily.

Sneap/snape

My friend Miley Connors, a Traveller of Wexford origin who used to deal in horses in his young days, used a very interesting old word in my presence not long ago. He pronounced it *snape*, but it is more often written as *sneap*. It means, he told me, to snub.

He has been sneaped quite a bit in his time, old Miley. His word is not cant, but an old word that was once used extensively before somehow falling on hard times and deemed to be slang. The word also had the meanings to pinch, to bite, to chill, benumb, starve, in the dialects of England, including Shakespeare's Warwickshire one. In *A Winter's Tale* the great man has: 'That may blow/No sneaping winds at home, to make us say/This is put forth too truly.' In *The Rape of Lucrece* we find the lovely passage: 'Like little frosts that sometimes threat the Spring,/To add a more rejoicing to the prime,/And give the sneaped birds more cause to sing.'

Snig

Gerry McCarthy from Glasnevin tells me that *snig*, noun and verb, is used in a hurling context in Waterford. As a noun it means a one-handed flick with the hurl. Poached goals are often got with a snig, or by snigging the ball over the goal-line.

I can only guess as to the origin of my correspondent's word. Would it be the English slang and dialect word meaning to steal? Kipling has: 'If you've ever snigged the washin' from the line,' in one of his barrack room ballads.

Sniggling

Michael Doorley sent me the slang word *sniggling* which he heard in his youth in Borrisokane, Co. Tipperary. 'The word means fishing for eels using a nine-inch long hook covered in earthworms,' he tells me. 'The hook was placed in crevices between rocks in the river or under bridges.'

The noun *sniggle* is found in many of the regional dialects of England. It means an eel. It is also found as *snig* in many places, but Co. Antrim is the only Irish location mentioned in the *English Dialect Dictionary*. In Cheshire a restless child was said to 'wriggle about like a snig in a bottle'. All over the English midlands, where they seem to be particularly fond of snigs, related words emerged, such as *snig-bag*, an eel bag; *snig-bellied*, said of a very thin person or animal; *snig-pie*, an eel pie. 'A snygge, a ele' is mentioned in a tract dating from 1483.

Mr Doorley's *sniggle*, 'to catch fish, especially eels', according to the *English Dialect Dictionary*, is commonplace from Scotland south to Devon, but there is no mention of Ireland. A Northamptonshire correspondent defined the verb as 'to lay baits for catching eels in their holes. Sometimes used metaphorically for inveigling or securing a person by stratagem.' Mr Doorley's old word is of unknown origin, I'm sorry to say, but it is good to know that it survives in Tipperary.

Snool

This word has a variety of meanings along the banks of Lough Neagh, where the lexicographer Lutton heard it in the early years of the twentieth century. It still thrives. Lutton glossed it as 'a mean, dastardly person; one who will stoop to anything, however low and dishonourable; one who will tamely submit to anything, however oppressive.' The word seems to be from the Scots *snule*; possibly a form of *snivel*. I note that the *Concise Ulster Dictionary* also gives *snool* as a verb: to cow, intimidate; make someone dispirited; to sulk, moan, complain. It also gives the adjective *snooly*, referring to a person who is always complaining. I wonder does another *snool*, a person who allows his or her hair to grow down over the eyes, and the related verb, come from a different source? It looks like it.

Snot

This word for nasal mucus is commonplace, but I've often wondered if the verb *to snot* is found outside Co. Wicklow. It means to fall flat on one's face or to bang one's face against a glass door, a not infrequent accident, I'm reliably informed. 'He really snotted himself when he fell.' I'm obliged to my daughter, Aifric, for this word.

Sough/sugh

This lovely old word for a hollow, murmuring sound, the sighing or moaning of the wind, a gentle murmur or hum, is alive and well in most northern counties. Carleton has it in *Fardorougha the Miser*: 'Nothing heard but the sugh of the mountain river.' Burns also had *sugh*: 'The clanging sugh of whispering wings is heard', he wrote in *The Brigs of Ayr*. Scott spelled it *sough* in *The Antiquary*: 'Amid the melancholy sough of the dying wind.' How it came to south-east Wexford I have no idea. Old Jack Devereux, God look to him, pronounced it *zough*; he was speaking of the zough of the sea between Kilmore Quay and the Saltee Islands on summer nights.

Oxford says that the word in all its forms was adopted into general literary use in the nineteenth century. Wordsworth used Donegal's *sugh*: 'Fain wail of eagle ... and pinewood's steady sugh.' As far as I know Chaucer was the first to use the word in literature. In the *Parliament of Foules* (c.1381) he speaks of hearing 'a swow that gan a-boute renne'.

As to origin, the word comes through Middle English from Old English *swegen*, equivalent to Low German *swogen*, groan, sound.

Sowl

A Waterford friend, Tom Power, sent me an interesting word recently: *sowl*. It means to pull by the ears. I had the word from Carne in south-east Wexford. Old Phil Wall used it, a man who was in his nineties when I met him in, as far as I remember, 1970. This word is common enough across the water from Scotland to Cornwall. Secondary meanings have been recorded by the *English Dialect Dictionary*, to chastise, to beat violently; to pull about roughly, to handle rudely, to tumble one's clothes. 'Sowl into him' was recorded in Lincolnshire.

These secondary meanings have not reached Ireland, as far as I know, but the first one I mentioned was known by Shakespeare. In *Coriolanus* he has: 'He'll go, he says, and sole the porter of Rome gates by th' eares.' Heywood, in *Love's Mistress*, written in 1636, used the word as well: 'Venus will sole me by the eares for this.' The word is also found in the dictionaries of Australian and New Zealand dialect and slang. Nobody knows the origin of the word.

Spadger/Spadge

An interesting word I heard in Cork not long ago was *spadger*. A woman in Blackpool called to her little son who was playing in the street, 'Come in to your tea, you little spadger!' Seán Beecher in his *Dictionary of Cork Slang* (1983) has *spadge*.

Spadger is a fanciful alteration of *sparrow*. It is an import from England; the *English Dialect Dictionary* has it from fourteen counties. Robinson's *Dialect of Leeds*, published in 1862, tells us that 'spadger pie is an article of diet occasionally'. Not any longer, I fancy.

Stales

I heard this word used by a wildfowler by the banks of the Slaney recently. *Stales*, he said, are decoys or lures used to attract birds. I have read that the word comes from the Old English *stalu*, a theft, or *stelan*, to steal, but Oxford disagrees. It is, in all probability, from Anglo-French *estale*, applied to a pigeon used to entice a hawk into a net. The word is of Germanic origin, it is thought. Compare the Old English *staelhrán*, decoy reindeer, and the Northumbrian *staello*, catching of fish. Think too of the German *stellvogel*, decoy bird. So much for the word's pedigree.

It has been used a lot in English literature ever since it first appeared in the famous glossary *Promptorium Parvulorum Sive Clericorum* about 1440: 'Stale: of fowlynge or byrdys takynge, *stacionaria*.'

The Tudors were very familiar with the word. Beaumont and Fletcher have it in *The Humorous Lieutenant*: 'stales to catch kites'. Sydney has it in *Arcadia*: 'But rather one bird caught served as a stale to bring I more.' Shakespeare used the word in both *The Taming of the Shrew* and in *The Tempest*, where he has: 'The trumpery in my house, go bring it hither,/For stale to catch those thieves.'

Staving

Yet another word for very drunk. This was sent to me by Mattie Cronin of Fossa, Killarney. Of unknown origin. The *English Dialect Dictionary* has it from Co. Antrim.

Steam

This is a Tuam schoolboy noun. It means fun. 'She's great steam,' means she's great fun. But *taking the steam* means, as the *Beginner's Dictionary* so delicately puts it, 'extracting the urine'.

Steeved/steevin

Steeved is an Ulster slang word for full of food. One can be *steeved* or *steeved up*. There is also the noun *steevin*, in Lutton's *Montiaghisms* as *steevan*, a heavy meal. This is the same word as the dockers' verb *steeve*, to stow a cargo.

They may be regarded as slang nowadays, but all these words have a pedigree. They come from the French *estiver*, corresponding to Italian *stivare*, to crowd, to pack tightly, from Latin *stipare*.

Stevin

I was in a pub, in the company of Councillor Leo Carthy of Lady's Island, in the Barony of Forth, Co. Wexford, when a young lady was asked to sing. As she cleared her throat rather shyly, a young fellow who had, perhaps, a drop too much taken, started up himself, only to be told in no uncertain manner by an old lady present, to sit down and shut up. 'Wait your stevin,' she said. He complied.

Stevin (it rhymes with Kevin) is an amazing survival. It came to Forth with the Anglo-Normans all those years ago, and its ultimate origin is the Old English *stefyn*, a period of time.

Strap

This pejorative word for a woman is probably from Irish *straip*, defined by Dinneen's dictionary as a harlot. Joyce used the word in Molly Bloom's soliloquy: '... you be damned, you lying strap.' More recently Tom Murphy has it in *Bailegangáire*: 'Pat went back to his strap of a widdy. An' was dead in six months.'

Strumble

Strumble is Mrs Annie Wall's word for straw. Master Green has the word as well, from Co. Longford Travellers.

Subowl/suból

Shelta for a bottle. *Suból a skai*, a bottle of water. Mrs Annie Wall's word. A perversion of Irish *buidéal.*

Swimmers and bricks

This is a Dungarvan, Co. Waterford, slang term for fish and chips.

Swurkin/swurkra/swurk

Swurkin is Shelta for a song. Mrs Annie Wall used to visit my home in Co. Wicklow occasionally and in a thank-you gesture for a cup of tea or a drop of whiskey she would give me Shelta words and sing me a *swurkin* or two. *Swurkra* is her word for a singer, and the verb is *swurk.*

Tack

One of the most interesting words I have heard in recent years is this *tack* I heard in Dungarvan, Co.

Waterford. 'God keep that tack from us', a farmer from Old Parish direction said of the foot-and-mouth plague. From the French *tac* this, 'a kind of rot among sheep; also a plague spot', according to Randle Cotgrave's *French-English Dictionary* of 1610. The French word is from the Latin *tactus*, found in the sense infectious, contagious disease.

Tallamacka/telemachus/tallymackey

It's quite a few years ago since Maichín Seoighe of Tankardstown, Kilmallock, Co. Limerick, wrote to me about one of his mother's words, *tallamacka*, which means a hullabaloo, clamour, noisy disagreement. Séamus Moylan found the word as *telemachus* in Tullogher, Co. Kilkenny, and John Rochford from Waterford heard it as *tallymackey* at the foot of the Comeraghs. A flood of letters came to me suggesting possible origins, including, needless to say, Telemachus, son of Odysseus and Penelope. I discarded them all and had given up the quest of searching for the etymology of the word when a letter arrived from the desk of the Rev. B.H. Sharp, at The Vicarage, Cymbach, near Aberdare, in Wales. He had heard of my search and wrote to tell me that he thought he had the answer to my problem. He is worth listening to. This is what he had to say:

'Tallamacka: would it have a religious connection? St Telemachos (his Greek name; Almachius in Roman Catholic calendars) was martyred in Rome about 400 AD. He was a monk from the east who sought to put an end to gladiatorial contests. One day he ran into the arena to separate the contestants. There was a hullabaloo and a half, and poor Telemachos was killed. Nobody is sure who killed him. Perhaps it was the mob who didn't want their fun ruined; perhaps it was the gladiators, on the orders of the city prefect who thought such scenes bad for business. Anyway, it is said that as a result of the affray the emperor Honorius abolished such barbarous shows. Did the saint give his name to the uproar?'

Well, what do you think?

Tear *(pr. tare)*

This particular *tear*, noun and verb, seems to be a native of Co. Cork. As a noun it means a hot bout of sexual play, stopping short of what Robert Burns called *houghmagandie* (q.v.). The young one in the Cork song *The Bould Thady Quill*, was suffering from a mysterious ailment. As the song goes: 'Oh mama,' says she, 'shure I know what will aise me, and cure this disaise that is certain to kill; give over your doctors and medical tratement, I'd rather one tear out of bould Thady Quill.'

Tear arse bread

This is what people in Carne, Co. Wexford, call home-made oaten bread. It is not made much any more. Leo Carthy gave me the word.

Threep

Shelta for a sup. *Threep a gawther*, a sup of drink; *threep a skai*, a sup of water.

Tickle-the-bricks

A cant or slang phrase for a sneaky person. It is generally considered Dublin slang, but I've heard it in other places in Leinster. (See *Go-by-the-wall*.)

Tober

Shelta for a road. A perversion of Irish *bóthar*, road. Master Green collected the phrase *Do the shades misli this tober*? – do the police patrol this road?

Tome

A Tuam slang adjective which means 'wonderful, fabulous, legendary' according to the *Beginner's Dictionary*.

Trig

'He had it won from the trig,' said an English commentator on Galileo's Epsom Derby win. A school friend of mine wrote to me about the word at the time, because this word *trig* was to us youngsters in New Ross, Co. Wexford, where I was bred, born and reared, the point at which we placed our leading knuckle when playing marbles. Captain Gross had an identical definition in his *Dictionary of the Vulgar Tongue* back in 1795.

By *trig* the race commentator meant, of course, the beginning, the starting stalls in this case. I heard this word for the starting line in a Donegal rural athletic meeting. Simmons's 1890 glossary of Donegal words has it; so has *The Concise Ulster Dictionary*. From Northumberland the *English Dialect Dictionary* recorded: '"Toe the trig", keep your toe on the starting line. "Come back to the trig" is shouted when a false start has been made.'

As to the origin of this word from my schooldays, Oxford says it is not sure. It does speculate, however, that as the Dutch word *trekker* has become *trigger* in English, it is conceivable that the Dutch *trekken*, to draw a line, might become *trig*.

Tyke

I've heard this word used in a pejorative fashion in many places in Leinster and south Ulster of a young hooligan or of a tiresome lout. I once heard Patrick Kavanagh call a barman who had refused him a pint 'a bloody oul' tyke'. The word is in common use in Scotland and in England, and its use in Shetland for the common otter gives a clue to its origin: the Old Norse *tik*, a bitch. Langland used the word in *Piers Plowman*: 'but under tribut and taillage as tykes and cherles'.

Ucks

This is a Cork city word for an apple core. Leslie Matson, teacher and scholar, sent me the gloss, 'Have you on the ucks', which means 'Save the apple core for me' in standard English. As to origin, I'm afraid I'm stuck.

Wabblin' brush

Derry city slang for a shaving brush.

Waddler

Waddler is Shelta for a duck. Master Green gave us this from Longford.

Wart

This is Shelta for 'one'. It is a corruption of Irish *amháin*, one.

Weatherby's (not in)

Weatherby's is the official thoroughbred horse register. The late Willie Evans from Greystones once told me that to say that somebody was not in Weatherby's was to imply that he was not a thoroughbred; that he was a bastard, not to put a tooth in it. The more genteel of the old horse people used the phrase, women especially.

Wersh

Wersh cooking means insipid fare. I've heard this adjective used figuratively in Donegal, just as Scott used it in *Old Mortality*: 'The Worcester man was but wersh parritch [porridge]; neither gede to fry, boil nor sup cauld.'

Simmonds, in his south Donegal glossary of 1890 defines *wersh* as 'weak, delicate, lacking in stamina'. Palsgrave's dictionary of 1530 has, 'Werysshe as meat is that is nat well tayste.'

The word is probably a contracted form of *wearish*, an obsolete (I think) form of late Middle English *werische*, of obscure origin.

Wheeker/wheek/wheekin/wheek maleeries

As far as I know these words are not found in Ireland south of the border. *You Don't Say* has it.

It is, according to Willie O'Kane, 'something excellent or outstanding. "That new goalie is a real wheeker," means that he or she is very good. Anything that impresses the speaker, be it a work of art, a motor car or a pedigree bull, can be described as a wheeker.'

The *Concise Ulster Dictionary* also has *wheek*, verb, to snatch. This is in the nineteenth-century glossaries, as is the adjective *wheekin*, very good, smashing. I love *wheekmaleeries*, 'ornamental flourishes of the pen', such as you might see on Saturday night pub cheques or in Plantaganet documents.

All onomatopoeic words from Scotland.

Widow's memories

Tuam slang for sausages.

Wigger

This is Dublin slang for a sexy young woman. It is an old word; indeed it arrived in English way back in the thirteenth century, when it was adapted from either Middle Low Geman or Middle Dutch *wiggelen*. It is, as you may have guessed, related to the verb *wig*, to waggle, or shake, and also to *wiggle*. I was surprised to find the great *English Dialect Dictionary* say that *wigger* was now obsolete except in Shetland; it obviously had never heard of Coolock or its wiggers.

Withershin

Now there's a quare word for you from Ulster. The *Concise Ulster Dictionary* has recorded it, and a correspondent from Bangor, Co. Down, Robert Blair, has heard the word in the Ards Peninsula and in a townland near Cullybackey in Co. Antrim. It is an adverb meaning in a direction contrary to the sun's course; from right to left; generally, in the wrong direction.

The word is found as *withershins* in Scotland, Northumberland, Lancashire, Shropshire, and Cornwall. Scott, in *Waverly*, glosses the word: 'Old Highlanders will still make the *deasil* around those whom they wish well to. To go around a person in the opposite direction, or wither-shins, is unlucky, and a sort of incantation.' (*Deasil* is Gaelic *deiseal*, to the right.)

From Fergusson's charming *Rambles* (1884) comes the information that 'to turn a boat against the sun, or withershins, at the beginning of a voyage is considered unfavourable.' He was speaking of Orkney. The same notion was recorded from Lancashire fishermen. In Black's *Folk Medicine* (1883) we find this: 'On the first three Wednesdays of May children suffering from mesentric disease are dipped three times in Chapelle Uny "widderschynnes", and widderschynnes dragged three times around the well.'

The word has been in Scottish literature since 1513, when Douglas wrote this in his *Eneados*: 'And on the bak half writis widdirsinnis Plentie of lesyngis.'

The origin of the word is the Middle Low German *weddersins*, which means, literally, 'against the direction'.

Wobbler

This is Mrs Annie Wall's Shelta for a goat. It is a perversion of Irish *gabhar*, goat.

Yewr

A Shelta word of Miley Connors'. Possibly from Romani *yora*, *ora*, a watch or a clock; an hour.

Yokin

This is one of Dungannonman Willie O'Kane's words. He describes it as follows: 'a spell of work; the period during which the horses were yoked and working was a "yokin". At mealtimes they would be unyoked and allowed to rest or graze for a while. The term has been widened to describe any period of farmwork; "there will be a couple of yokins in this job", i.e. two periods of working with a lunchbreak in between.'

This word is found in Scotland and in Northern England. It is glossed by the *English Dialect Dictionary* as 'the period during which a ploughman and his team work at a stretch; any period of long, steady work done at a stretch'. The word's immediate origin, *yoke*, is itself Germanic in origin. Consider the Old Saxon *juk*, the Middle Dutch *juk* and *jok*.

Yortlin

This Ulster word means, according to Willie O'Kane's Dungannon glossary *You Don't Say*, 'a small, chirpy person, usually a child. Someone cheeky or forward, or in some way annoying, might be dismissed as *a bit of a yortlin*.' *Yort* is English dialectal for 'yard'; could a *yortlin(g)* be a young person who hangs around farmyards, being cheeky? I'm guessing.

Yorum

Shelta for milk. Master Green has the word from Longford Travellers.